THE FEARLESS FEMALE LEADER

A Proven Process to Speak Up, Be Heard,
and Have an Even Greater Impact

SHERYL KLINE, M.A. CHPC

Printed in the United States of America.

Hardcover ISBN: 978-1-960876-84-3

Paperback ISBN: 978-1-960876-85-0

Library of Congress number has been applied for and is pending.

For more information or to book an event, contact: info@sherylkline.com http://www.sherylkline.com

First Edition: February 2025

All names in case studies and stories have been changed to maintain confidentiality.

Dedicated to those who believe that one woman
can change the world.

****

Also, for my mother Barbara and my father Cecil,
with love.

SHERYL KLINE, M.A. CHPC

Foreword

I have always believed that if you don't know where you are going, you have no shot at getting there. Seems logical, right? If you set out in your car and you don't know your destination, you will just meander. For anything you undertake in life, you should first set out your destination — what is your objective, and where do you want to end up?

What I like about Sheryl's proven process in Fearless Female Leadership, though, is that it is not just about guiding you to land on a destination and chart your course to get there. It is much more. It is about becoming fearless in what's possible for you, building the confidence to see it through, and then learning how to gain buy-in from those who can really champion you and get behind your efforts. When you set out the destination and begin to build your vision, you'll not just learn how to make it yet another milestone — you'll learn to think bigger. You'll learn how to paint that vision in Technicolor and build your story, not just about what is achievable but what wild success will look like.

I will share a story of a time this worked for me. I was leading the Windows client business at Microsoft when we were just about to release Windows Vista. You may recall that Vista was not very well received in the enterprise market as it had poor application compatibility and poorly executed value over its well- adopted predecessor, Windows XP. My job was to grow the business despite this headwind, so I worked with my team to define wild success not just for Windows Vista but for the next version we would embark on. This meant marrying our fate and success to both versions while at the same time knowing that absolute success for the product about to be released was not achievable. We made this release a milestone in our journey to wild success. We said at the end of the two- step release that we will have redefined what security, manageability, and application compatibility deliver in the enterprise, and we will have usurped the place of Windows XP in 90 percent of all enterprises. We painted that vision with customer quotes, analyst quotes, and statistics. We dreamed up customer milestones and internal measurements we planned to blow out of the water. We did it as a team. We forged through the setbacks because we had clarity, we had courage, and we had conviction. We also built a cadre of support throughout the organization of sponsors and allies who all felt vested in the approach, the vision, and the success. I credit that bold exercise to create our vision as a key to our success. We not only achieved but exceeded all those measures within a four-year period. Without that level of bold, fearless focus, it would not have been possible.

But it is not enough to dream big. You also have to know how to execute, and how to build the roadmap to get to where you want to go. And you need to build your fan base along the way.

My secret sauce is to enlist people in the journey. I share my vision when it is literally half-baked. Most people will hold out on sharing a plan until they believe it is 80–100 percent complete. That way, they can answer all the questions people might have. I find this to be a faulty approach. You want people to be invested in the outcome and to feel like they chose to jump on board and had a hand not only in the execution but in the planning process. So, I invite people to engage very early and often. When they sign up to deliver pieces of it, I hold them accountable.

Another important part of creating success is, I believe, that empowerment and accountability live hand in hand. You want those with whom you work to be empowered. Your success is dependent on your willingness to give up control to others. You can't be a leader if you have no followers. People follow you because of your vision and because they feel successful themselves when they work with you. You want and need people to work with you.

If you want to learn how to develop that level of clarity, along with the courage and conviction to carry it forward, I recommend you read this book. Sheryl's Fearless Female Leadership framework will help you surpass your own wildest expectations.

Gavriella Schuster

Former Corporate Vice President, Microsoft | Diversity, Equity & Inclusion Top Voice LinkedIn |Global Business Executive | Board Director | TEDx Speaker | Digital Transformation Leader | Empowering Allies & Women www.gavriellaschuster.com #allies

"What I want young women and girls to know is:
You are powerful, and your voice matters."

— *Kamala Harris*

SHERYL KLINE, M.A. CHPC

SHERYL KLINE, M.A. CHPC

Table of Contents

CHAPTER 18 OVERVIEW   319

Introduction

My grandmother's name was Esther. At the age of 14, she was taken out of her public school in San Francisco by her father to do administrative work in the family's business, Golden Gate Iron and Steel. Esther loved learning and she would not allow her fate to be sealed, so she pleaded for her father to allow her to stay in school. Her desperate requests and those of her teachers who recognized her curiosity and hard work fell on deaf ears. Harry Schuster's decision was final.

Esther wondered why her brothers were not only allowed but encouraged to eventually go on to Stanford and receive their engineering degrees. Unfair or not, my grandmother did not let this injustice consume her for long. She continued her education anyway, on her own. She studied many subjects and was particularly interested in business and economics. As the years went by, my grandmother got to know the iron and steel business by doing her secretarial work, by listening, and by asking her father questions.

Esther came to her father one day, concerned about the employees of Golden Gate Steel. She'd been thinking about how to protect their jobs and, ultimately, their families in the event of a downturn in the economy. Esther didn't stop there, she'd even dreamt of how Golden Gate Steel could grow and provide more jobs, and she eventually got up the courage to knock on her father's large, heavy mahogany office door. Her father waved her to come in, listened to her ideas for how to protect and even grow the company's workforce, and exclaimed, "Your brothers have an education from Stanford and can advise me. Esther, you have your job to do here. Please go do it."

At the time, Golden Gate Steel was still bustling from business rebuilding following the 1906 San Francisco earthquake and from riding the coattails of a strong post-WWI economy. My grandmother studied history, the newspapers, and economic research and noted the roaring 1920s seemed to be taking a turn. Years later, Esther tried again to warn her father of what could be coming and why it may be a good idea to diversify the business and try new things to hedge against a possible downturn. She was met with the same response, "Esther, you have a job to, now please go do it. Your brothers will advise me if there's anything to worry about."

As the Great Depression eventually became imminent, Golden Gate Iron and Steel suffered the economic blows that so many other businesses endured. Esther's father was forced to lay off a majority of the workforce and eventually sold the company for a fraction of what it was worth during its strongest years. Would the story of Golden Gate Iron and Steel be different if my grandmother got to go to Stanford or some other college like her brothers, or if her voice was heard, valued, and respected? We'll never know. In my heart, I feel it would.

My grandmother went on to have two daughters: my mother, Barbara, and her sister, Janet. While having a seemingly happy and comfortable childhood in an upper-middle-class home, my mother, Barbara, suffered from bipolar disorder after I was born. As I write this, it makes me wonder what part the pressure of being a parent played in exacerbating her disease. Perhaps it was worsened by my brother who is 10 years my senior. He endured 15–20 years struggling with alcohol and drug addiction and took the rest of us with him on this chaotic, dangerous, and disruptive soul-altering journey. Or, maybe it was discovering, to her surprise, that she could have a daughter after many years of trying and giving up.

I've often wondered if her struggles with mental illness were exacerbated by how purposeless she often felt. My mom's desire was to become a conservationist, specifically for endangered owls, which held a special place in her heart. She researched the endangered owls endlessly and had countless owl pins and figurines as constant reminders of how she felt connected to them. When I'd ask her what was so special about owls, she'd reply that they were mysterious and incredibly smart. Perhaps she couldn't even explain why they were special to her but protecting them seemed part of her life's purpose.

One morning, while we sat around our small round breakfast table, my mother began talking about the owls. My father looked up from his oatmeal and said, "Barbara, who are you to save a species of owls?

You went in one door and out the other of UC Berkeley." My mother's face fell, and she stopped talking about this passionate part of her life. The one thing, other than her children, that she deeply cared about had been diminished, reduced to crumbs instead of a cake.

My father's words of criticism were delivered with a crushing blow to an already susceptible psyche. Without the tools and support to be a fearless female leader, my mother accepted his words of "not good enough" as truth, and she gave up on her dream and plan to help the owls. Sadly, my mother passed away at the age of 69. Just a few months later, many of the species of owls she was tracking were placed on a "severely endangered" list.

Have you ever witnessed generational messages of "not good enough" and considered how it's impacted you?

It's only been recently that I've given myself some grace around taking over five decades to break through the conscious and subconscious generational indoctrinations I grew up with. I wouldn't say I'm "cured," but I'm aware and willing to look fear, doubt, unworthiness, and feeling like an imposter in the face, honor them, even thank them, and keep going.

I wasn't always able to do this.

From fourth to ninth grade, I attended a small, private, and highly competitive school in the East Bay of San Francisco. In hindsight, it was not the best place for me, but at the time, I loved my school.

To me, this school was my ticket to be happier than my mother (I didn't understand her bipolar disorder when I was younger, but I noticed she was sad a lot of the time) and not be like my older brother, who struggled with substance abuse.

Getting good grades did not come easy to me. I always felt like I was capable, but I had to work five times harder than everyone else. I didn't understand why I excelled at philosophy, literature, and writing while chemistry and any logic- based math took Herculean amounts of work and seemingly endless tutors. But even if it was going to take five times the work, it was worth it to me for the promise of a future that was calm, safe, and happy.

Sometimes it was hard to concentrate and study in my unpredictable home. When I was in elementary school, despite our nice neighborhood and white picket fence, I never knew what to expect. After school, I'd often walk into the family room and find my brother passed out on the floor. Other times, I'd be asleep in my bedroom and smell smoke. Was the house burning down? Should I run down the hall and wake up my parents to ensure they can get out in time? I'd lie in my bed frozen with fear. One night I woke up at two o'clock to the smell of smoke and the sound of the television buzzing. I got up the courage to peek down the stairs to see if we were in imminent danger. My brother was asleep on the couch, and the electric burner in the kitchen had been left on with a pot of billowing smoke.

While sleep eluded me many nights, it wasn't as bad as the chaos that ensued during the day. There was yelling, pleading, and threatening from my brother for more money to fuel his addiction. The routine was that my brother would yell at my mom, and my dad would yell a t m y brother. Then, d o o r s w o u l d slam.

Thankfully, my brother would always leave, at least for a while.

Despite this chaos, I was determined to do well in school. I made a fort using my bed sheet so I could study under my desk. It made me feel safe and seemed to help buffer the yelling. I spent many hours a week under my desk, sometimes with a flashlight at night, studying vocabulary flashcards, doing my math, learning Latin, and working on projects.

In the fifth grade, when I got called into Principal Harris's office, I got excited! Maybe she'd noticed how hard I'd been working and called me down to praise me. Then I saw my parents sitting in the corner. My tall and muscular dad sat in his baggy khakis, short-sleeve white three-button shirt, and his favorite Members Only jacket. His legs were crossed so I could see his tube socks halfway up his leg with two green stripes. My mom was wearing a conservative blush-colored dress, and her hair was washed and styled, which was unusual. As I looked at Mrs. Harris, with her curly hair and her narrow brown eyes peering over her spectacles, my excitement turned to concern, then dread.

"Sheryl," Mrs. Harris said. "You've been working very hard, and you're doing pretty well with your grades. Unfortunately, with the near-perfect standards of our school, you're not doing well enough to remain a student here." Her pronouncement knocked the wind out of me as if I'd received a gut punch from a giant. I was 10 years old, and I felt that my fate was sealed.

I looked to my parents to speak up for me and tell Mrs. Harris that I was good enough and that I worked extremely hard for those As and Bs. But they didn't. We took her words as truth and left. Once we were outside Mrs. Harris's door, my dad leaned down and told me, "Sheryl, it's only October. You have the rest of the school year to prove yourself."

I thought that was great news! I gave up all my after-school activities, checked on my mom when I got home and worked longer and harder under my tent desk. The following year, in late June, after school was out, my father called me into the kitchen. It was a Sunday morning, and he was making scrambled eggs and Vienna sausages, my favorite at the time. He was wearing blue plaid pajama bottoms and a white V-neck undershirt. I looked up at him as he stirred the eggs. What he told me next left me speechless, numb, empty, and hopeless.

"Sheryl, you won't be going back to your school in the fall."

I grew up devouring everything about the Olympics. I thought from a young age that if you worked harder than anyone else, you'd win. Why wasn't my hard work good enough for me to "win" and stay at my school? I was doing the work and getting good—but apparently not good enough— grades. Staying in this school was my Olympics, and I felt like I was working longer and harder than everyone else, only to fall short of the finish line. Did Mrs. Harris really hold the power to decide my destiny? At the time, I thought the answer was yes.

I ended up transferring to a local public school where I stayed through high school before heading off to college. My initial degree was in English at the University of Oregon in Eugene. I loved literature and writing, but my career path was unclear. During most of my time in Eugene, from 1984 to

1988, I lived across the street from Hayward Field, home to many Olympic trials, Prefontaine Classic track meets, NCAA Championships, and various other notable track and field events. My sorority sisters and I would either sit on the roof of our sorority house or walk across the street to watch the NCAA track and field finals; international track meets, and the 1988 Olympic trials. We walked down the bleachers to stand at the hip-high fence that separated the spectators from the world-class athletes and current and future Olympians.

One sunny afternoon in 1988, I saw Carl Lewis jogging by. I recognized him after watching him set world records and win gold medals in track and field at the 1984 Olympics. In person, it appeared his legs were impossibly long with a layer of skin over pure muscle. I was giddy with excitement seeing this world- renowned athlete in person. In his career that spanned from 1979 to 1996, Carl won nine Olympic gold medals, one Olympic silver medal, and 10 World Championships medals, including eight gold. Shortly after I saw Carl compete at Hayward Field, he went on to win two gold medals and one silver medal at the 1988 Seoul Olympics. While watching Carl accept his 1988 Olympic gold medals, a question lodged itself in my brain. Who gets to decide who's good enough? Who chose Carl and decided he was good enough to be one of the most decorated and accomplished track and field athletes of all time? Who decided he was good enough to also be drafted into the NBA and the NFL without having ever played those sports in high school?

It was not who you might think.

Evelyn L. Lewis not only believed in her son Carl and his three siblings, but she also showed them that we are only limited by what we think is possible, even if we are the first to attempt something that may seem crazy or unsurmountable or when others are telling us it can't be done.

According to the obituary published by Mabrie Memorial Mortuary, Evelyn was born in Gadsden, Alabama, the sixth of nine children, and was so skinny everyone called her "Chicken Legs." During her senior year of high school, she competed in a track meet at Tuskegee Institute, where she caught the eye of the university's coach, who soon recruited her. She became the first member of her family to attend college. Evelyn made the honor roll and became the schools number 1 hurdler. Her accomplishments were still notable in 1985 when she was inducted into the Tuskegee University

Athletic Hall of Fame, according to a news release from the school about her passing.

In 1951, Evelyn went to Buenos Aires, Argentina, for the first Pan American Games. "Who would have thought that a skinny little Black girl from Gadsden would have traveled to Buenos Aires and even met Evita Peron," she would later ask. (Thornton, 2023).

Evelyn later broke the US record for the women's 80-meter hurdles and had her sights set on the 1952 Olympic Games in Helsinki, Finland. By then, she was one of the top three hurdlers in the world, but an injury before the Olympic trials kept her off the team.

According to a 2023 story published in the Gadsden Times, Evelyn and her husband accepted teaching jobs and initially settled in Montgomery, where they welcomed sons Mack and Cleve, then moved to Birmingham, where Carl and Carol were born. They lived in Alabama during some of the biggest events of the Civil Rights Movement, participating in the Montgomery bus boycott and providing support to Dr. Martin Luther King Jr. and his family. They attended King's first church, Dexter Avenue Baptist, where he baptized Mack and Cleve.

When they lived in Birmingham, the family faced race-related issues every day. According to the obituary, Evelyn remembered taking the long way home to avoid passing an amusement park that wouldn't admit Blacks so she wouldn't have to explain to her older sons why they couldn't go there.

Evelyn was one of the first Black teachers in the school district. She began coaching field hockey, later coached track and field, and was involved in other programs for girls. When the school wouldn't start a track program for girls, she and her husband started one of their own, the Willingboro Track Club, in 1969. She taught and coached until her retirement in 1985.

Evelyn decided what she was capable of despite unimaginable challenges and setbacks. She decided to be the first in her family to earn a college degree and eventually her master's degree, to be an international track and field champion, to become the first woman of color to teach in her school district, and to imbue her children with the knowledge that they are truly limitless. And when it was Carl Lewis's turn to make decisions for himself, he chose himself, too.

My questioning of who gets to decide who's good enough, especially with regard to world-class athletes and

SHERYL KLINE, M.A. CHPC

Olympians continued to grow, and I went on to study and get my master's degree in applied sports psychology at the University of Southern California. I focused my research on Olympic athletes. Did someone choose them? Once they arrived at the Olympics after training for years, if not decades, how did they perform under such immense pressure? The last question was especially vexing for me because I was not able to perform under pressure. I reflected again on my last year at private school when I worked hard and learned the necessary material, but there was so much riding on my performance that my emotions made this knowledge inaccessible.

After researching and working with some of the best athletes in the world, I learned that world-class performers like Evelyn and Carl Lewis choose themselves, and they decide that they are good enough. Eventually, I had the honor of working with world-class soccer players, Olympic-level equestrian show jumpers, track and field athletes, and elite tennis players. All of them had something in common: They were keenly aware of what lies in their heart and in their gut, what they wanted to accomplish, and they believed it was possible and took consistent action. They kept going when the road was difficult or when the outlook was bleak. They failed, learned, and tried again. They were fueled by an invisible power that's accessible to all of us.

These world-class performers encountered resistance, setbacks, and thoughts of giving up, skipping practice, and cracking under pressure, which could erase years or decades of work. Also, what they possessed in talent, work ethic, and audacity, they sometimes lacked in mental toughness and emotional agility. This could make it challenging to recover quickly from setbacks and to remain confident even when plagued by injury or crushing defeats.

Helping others to unlock their potential inspired me and lit me up with excitement. I wanted to help these athletes get better quicker and to be able to perform under pressure since that skill eluded me as a young person. This career was extraordinary and fun. I learned the science behind human performance and how our mindset is the driver of our belief system, our actions, and ultimately our destiny. I had a window into the thinking of those who chose themselves, who decided they were good enough to be the best, and who dedicated themselves to accomplishing what many others thought impossible. It truly opened my eyes to the limitless nature of human potential and the power of our minds to make it happen.

In 2015, after having worked with world-class athletes and Olympians for almost 20 years, I came to a fork in the road in my career, and I'm forever grateful for the opportunity, discomfort, and uncertainty that shook me out of my comfort zone. Thanks to a dear friend who was persistent and who saw something in me that I didn't see in myself at the time, I was presented with an amazing yet uncomfortable opportunity.

Amy Bunszel, an executive vice president of AEC design at Autodesk, asked if I'd like to be on a panel that Autodesk was hosting with Google Ventures on mental toughness for women in tech. My first response was, "Thank you for thinking of me, but no thank you." After all, why would I be on a panel in front of amazing, accomplished women in tech while sandwiched between a 30-under-30 go-getter and an executive coach to a who's who of Silicon Valley? Nope. Not me. That was an arena that I had yet to see myself in.

The truth is, I was scared. Up until this point, I'd helped the best in the world, who happened to be very young adults, to master their mindset and ability to perform under pressure, but I had not granted myself permission to be the best.

The feeling was one of excitement, and every cell in my body was saying yes, but my head stepped in with, *"You are absolutely not ready nor equipped for this."* Sound familiar? Most of us have experienced this at one time or another, which is completely normal. I've since learned to pay more attention to how I feel when making decisions rather than what I think I'm capable of.

This was an opportunity to look fear and doubt in the face and say yes to something I was excited about but didn't feel quite ready for. After interviewing over 100 influential and prolific female leaders, I've learned that this is a quality of a Fearless Female Leader, so I'll be excited to share more about this with you in the coming chapters.

Thankfully, my friend Amy was persistent, and I eventually said yes. I granted permission to myself. I decided I was good enough, and the preparation began. After two decades of researching and working with world-class athletes and Olympians, I knew what to do to prepare. How to look fear, doubt, and uncertainty in the face, make peace with them, and then use them to fuel my best performance. I am forever grateful for this opportunity and for Amy's belief in me. The event was a smash success. My content was well received, and I ended up working with one of the attendees to help her negotiate and receive funding for her company after she previously (and understandably) cracked under the pressure of approaching venture capitalists.

The Fearless Female Leadership framework you will learn in this book was born from my work with Olympians who achieved the seemingly impossible, from my own experience facing my fears, and from helping those female teach leaders that day in 2015 to influence under pressure and gain buy-in from key stakeholders.

Within months of participating on the Autodesk/Google Ventures panel, I decided. I decided that no one needed to choose me. No one needed to tell me if I was good enough. I decided to choose myself. I decided that every current and future leader deserved to know how to be mentally tough and how to perform under pressure, not just the elite few. I developed the Fearless Female Leadership framework to do just that.

I began donating my time and content to Kimberly Bryant's Black Girls Code and to Reshma Saujani's Girls Who

Code, helping female and emerging leaders become fearless and go from feeling silenced, overlooked, or disregarded to becoming heard, valued, and highly influential agents of change.

After having the honor of coaching, advising, and consulting for some of the most prolific and influential female leaders in San Francisco, Silicon Valley, and across the country, I noticed a frustrating gap and roadblock to them having their ultimate impact. While already confident and highly influential, some were not being heard, valued, and respected enough by their leadership. To add a valuable tool to these leaders' already stocked toolbelt, I became obsessed with becoming well-versed in FBI hostage negotiation and expanded my existing framework to include these tactics. These tools have proven invaluable in helping leaders have a louder voice at the table, gain buy-in from their leaders, and push initiatives forward.

Since creating the Fearless Female Leadership framework, I've been entrusted to lead teams at Google Ventures, Autodesk, Oracle, VMware, State Street Global Advisors, Bank of America, and Jabra, to name a few. Every leader, at every experience level, has a voice that matters and deserves to be heard, valued, and respected by their leadership.

In many cases, I partnered with these amazing leaders to help empower their emerging female leaders and pave the way for continued success. I began leading cohorts of emerging leaders through the same proven process that my executive clients went through. But it still wasn't enough. "If only the women in our company could all experience the transformation I have had," they'd say. Since there is only one of me and not an unlimited budget, I said yes once again to a crazy idea: Creating an enterprise digital platform for the Fearless Female Leader framework.

Gavriella Schuster, former corporate vice president at Microsoft, board member to too many companies to list, and creator of the enterprise program Allies, introduced me to Rich Cannon, a former Microsoft colleague and current CEO at Rali. Rali is a behavioral change platform founded by Larry Mohl, former chief learning officer of American Express and Motorola.

Partnering with Rali to create an enterprise digital program for the Fearless Female Leadership enterprise digital edition was exciting but scary initially. I'd be spending months working on the curriculum design, traveling to Atlanta from San Francisco to film on set with multiple cameras and a full crew, and writing checks that would make my bookkeeper's head spin. After all, I'm not Esther Perel filming MasterClass! This decision was out of my comfort zone on many different levels, but every ounce of my being told me to do it. And I did.

Like most people, I don't love being uncomfortable, but I believe wholeheartedly that discomfort is necessary to grow and have the impact we are meant to have. Of the more than 100 interviews I've done with some of the most influential and prolific female leaders in San Francisco, Silicon Valley, and across the country on my podcast, almost all of them have spoken about their willingness to embrace being uncomfortable. In other words, they look back fondly and with gratitude for the times when they said yes to opportunities that they did not feel ready or qualified for. World-class leaders feel doubt and fear, but they decide to have faith in themselves and take action anyway.

For me, recently creating the Fearless Female Leader Table of 12 Peer Advisory and Mastermind cohort, for example, was uncomfortable at first. I brought together some of the most prolific and powerful heart-centered female executives and former executives to amplify and compound their impact. I found myself grappling with conflicting feelings and messages. Sometimes, my body felt like the peer advisory mastermind was a "Hell yes! It's time!" while my mind was apprehensive. Who am I to bring together such powerful women currently or formerly leading at the highest level with over 300 years of combined experience? That question paralyzed me until I flipped it. Who am I to not take action on something that could compound the impact, support, and joy of 12 prolific and heart-centered female leaders?

I embody what you're about to learn: How to gain clarity on what's next, how to synthesize fear and doubt to put a plan into place, and how to influence others to champion your efforts.

Whether I'm coaching one female executive, leading a cohort of 20 to 100, or speaking from a stage in front of thousands at conferences such as Women of Silicon Valley, CREW Network Convention, Women of the Channel, or Microsoft's Women in Cloud, the message is the same. Your voice matters, and you can learn how to influence others to have an even louder voice at the table and make a more profound and lasting impact.

Hear that again: Your voice matters. What's in your heart matters, and we are at a time in history when your leadership is needed more than ever. It's time to raise our awareness of what lights us up, what makes us feel alive, but also a little fearful. Where is the edge of our comfort zone? Where do we need just a little more support, new tools, and encouragement to access our highest sense of leadership and biggest impact? You'll learn to answer all these questions in this book.

My vision for you is that you understand and believe that you're truly limitless. The only one who gets to decide the impact and joy that you'll have in your career and in your life is YOU. You're only limited by what you can see for yourself and by what you feel worthy of receiving. For nearly half my life, I didn't understand, believe, or have a proven process to guide me. Now I do, and so do you. You have a proven process based on two decades of research and applied work to help you uncover and access the leadership gifts already inside you. If you've ever felt like you are capable of more or have dreamed of having an even greater voice, this book is for you.

If your gut or your heart has whispered for you to speak up, throw your hat in the ring, dream bigger, or make a bold request, this book is for you. If you're thinking, "Hell yes! I'm ready to be heard and valued more," you are in the right place!

What's next for you is your figurative Olympics, and you will be learning a proven process that will give you the tools to:

1. Gain clarity for your next level of impact.

2. Build the confidence to achieve it.

3. Influence and gain buy-in so those in power can provide a tailwind to amplify your voice.

Let's take a brief look at each of these steps:

Clarity: Chart Your Path

In the Clarity chapter, we'll look at how clarity can be fluid, elusive, exhilarating, and agonizing. Whether deciding on a major life or career shift, trying to decide what's next in a current role, or pinpointing the desired outcome and preparation needed for an upcoming important conversation, clarity is key to designing and preparing for your best outcome as well as the joy that comes along with knowing you're congruent with your highest sense of passion and purpose.

Gaining clarity is similar to creating a path to ascend a mountain whose peak touches the sky. As world-class performers, though, we get to start at the top and work our way back down the mountain to the present day. Sometimes, we may decide to climb a different mountain or take a different route. If we can learn to own how we shift, make changes, and do the work, we can stay on our path to peak performance, contribution, and joy. In the Clarity chapter, you'll learn how to look inward to where your answers lie. You will be guided to tap into the power of your past, which may have provided great strength for you or may have clouded, even disarmed, your vision of yourself over the years. Either way, you'll uncover and benefit from the wisdom, strength, and power that your life experiences have to share by looking through a window that was previously hazy or completely covered.

The Clarity chapter consists of four sections: Integrity, Legacy, Success Roadmap™, and Moments. You'll learn how to gain high-level and aspirational clarity to serve as your internal driver, your personal North Star. You'll explore the legacy you would like to create or how you'd like to be remembered as a Leader.

And finally, you'll learn how to achieve clarity on how to show up for the moments that matter most. Just like an Olympic athlete practices for many years, if not decades, for moments that determine if she wins a gold medal, your experience and what you are trying to achieve are no less important. Your ideal outcome begins with clarity around what's next for you and how you'd like things to turn out.

Confidence: Own Your Shift

In the Confidence chapter, you'll learn how to own your shift from your amazing accomplishments up to this point to having an even bigger voice, impact, and buy-in from those who can champion your efforts. Similar to reaching the peak of a majestic and sometimes complex mountain, rising up to your next level of impact, whether via a major shift in your career or by projecting a bigger voice with your leadership, can evoke new emotions that throw us off our game or tempt us to pull back, even quit. These emotions can be like facing a garden snake on a trail that's supposed to be harmless, causing us to turn back because it feels like encountering a terrifying 600-pound gorilla.

I'll guide you through proven Olympic-level strategies to raise your awareness of the emotions that are serving you and the ones that are not. You'll be guided through a framework that will help you gain power and strength from emotions that previously disarmed your progress. You'll learn to transform the gorilla back into the harmless garden snake and eventually into a helpful guide.

As you ascend your mountain, you'll need the confidence to prepare mentally and tactically for your successes, setbacks, and course corrections, as well as how to be your best when the pressure is on. The Confidence chapter comprises four sections: Internal Voice, Visual Optimization, Emotional Agility, and Practice. These four proven processes will help you prepare for when the road gets rough or difficult to maneuver so that you can keep making progress. Finally, we'll also cover one of the most important factors in building confidence, building your competence through deliberate practice. You'll learn how to look fear and doubt in the face and synthesize its power into rocket fuel rather than allowing it to slow you down, not speak up, or not get started in the first place.

Influence: Mobilize Allies

There is only so much we can accomplish alone. If our impact is to be grand, we'll need to influence those in power to help us.

In the Influence chapter, you'll learn a framework grounded in FBI-level negotiation research to help mentally and tactically prepare for crucial conversations and presentations or to make a big ask. Here is the runway that will unlock your ability to build even greater trust, safety, and respect, so you'll almost never hear a no.

The four sections in the Influence chapter are ECO, which is an acronym for developing empathy, curiosity, and optimism; Amplify, which is a trust- building framework; Challenge Builder, which is a template for how to powerfully position your ask; and Aspiration Articulator, which is how to cast a vision for a future desired outcome so it's clear in your mind and clear to the other person.

Fearless Is Not the Absence of Fear

Becoming fearless does not mean being without fear. By definition, fear is "an unpleasant emotion caused by the belief that someone or something is dangerous, likely to cause pain or a threat." From an evolutionary perspective, if our lives were truly in danger, say a sabertoothed tiger was getting ready to make us its dinner, fear could save our lives.

If we are to become Fearless Female Leaders, speak up for what we want and deserve, make big asks, gain buy-in from those in power who can champion our efforts, and have a bigger voice and impact, we must welcome and give thanks for fear as a guide that we are on our right path. It's where our heart and our gut meet our willingness to step outside our comfort zone and take consistent action, where our highest sense of contribution and joy lies.

We are at an inflection point in history where women's voices, especially those who have been further marginalized within our gender, must be heard, valued, and respected. It's time for women to return to power, to equalize the patriarchy, and to become fearless agents of change.

The Fearless Female Leadership framework is not just a proven process that's been used with dozens of female executives and their teams. By reading this book, you will be able to chart your path for what's next, build the confidence to believe in yourself and take consistent action, and then learn how to build strategic-based influence so you can gain buy-in from your leadership.

I look forward to having you join us. We will create momentum together to empower over one million women to be fearless female leaders! #FFL1MM

SHERYL KLINE, M.A. CHPC

CHAPTER 1

The Situation

There are incredible men and women who have dedicated their lives to equality and inclusion in the workplace, and progress is being made. However, according to the 2023 Lean In/McKinsey and Company Women in the Workplace study, "The story is both encouraging and frustrating." The study states that there have been gains for women in senior leadership roles, which serves as an example of what companies can achieve when there are focused efforts and an understanding of the problem.

The study goes on to debunk myths about women's workplace experiences and career advancement. A few of these myths cover old ground, but given the notable lack of progress, they warrant repeating. Across the corporate pipeline, women—and especially women of color—remain underrepresented.

However, there is a growing bright spot in senior leadership. Since 2015, the number of women in the C- suite has increased from 17 to 28 percent, and the representation of women at the VP and SVP levels has also improved significantly. These hard-earned gains are encouraging but fragile. Progress is slower for women at the manager and director levels, creating a weak middle in the pipeline and impacting the majority of women in corporate America. And the "Great Breakup" continues for director level women: They are leaving at a higher rate than in past years and at a notably higher rate than men at the same level. As a result of these two dynamics, there are fewer women in line for top positions.

Here are the key findings from the study:

- Women represent roughly one in four C- suite leaders, and women of color just one in 16.
- Women of color face the steepest drop- off in representation from entry-level to C-suite positions. As they move up the pipeline, women of color's representation drops by two-thirds.

While the institution of corporate America is changing, its progress is slow and up against many cultural, social, political, and generational headwinds.

The Fearless Female Leadership framework is a

SHERYL KLINE, M.A. CHPC

solution based on a proven process for women and the male allies who support them to dream even bigger and become highly influential in their leadership. It's also a companion for leaders to support and amplify the women in their organization and to help rising female talent get and stay in their company's pipeline. The result? Better engagement, retention, innovation, and profitability across your entire organization, according to a recent study in the Harvard Business Review, which spotlighted a study of nearly 5,000 companies in 100 countries. The study evaluated how leaders could accomplish the most important challenges that are necessary to do their jobs while remaining "good human beings." When ranked by their subordinates, "[Employees] said that women leaders versus male leaders are able to do hard things in a human way."

What is the value of these findings? According to this same study that also looked at key business outcomes and the gender of employees and leaders using many metrics, including job performance and job engagement, "Women leaders save their organizations $1.43 million for every 1,000 employees (assumes an average salary of $60,000). Layered on top of this are the savings for not having to replace a disengaged employee, which requires one-half to two times the employee's annual salary, or between $30,000 and $120,000 per employee." The business impact is clear.

This book is a guide for female leaders and emerging leaders to gain clarity on a bigger vision for themselves and what's possible, to build Olympic-level confidence to believe in themselves and what they're capable of, and finally to build FBI-like strategic influence, so they can gain buy-in from their leaders who can in turn champion their efforts.

Before we dig into the Clarity, Confidence, and Influence chapters, let's assess where you are today on your Fearless Female Leadership journey. Here's a brief assessment you can take now and again when you're done reading this book and have completed the exercises and tools I provide throughout. Again, you can answer right here in this book or download the assessment at https://bit.ly/3W1F3rS or use this QR code:

Please answer all questions based on a scale of 1 - 10.

1 = "Nope / Not So Much --- 10 = "Yes! / I Got This"

1. I feel clear about my message, mission, and area of unique genius.

2. When speaking to my leadership, I feel heard, valued, and respected.

3. I always speak up when I have something important to contribute.

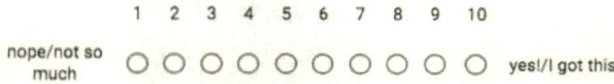

4. Prior to crucial conversations and high-stakes meetings, I am calm and confident.

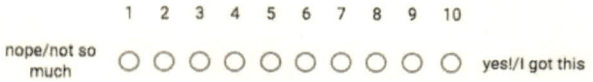

5. **If I had a magic wand and could not fail, my biggest dream in the next 12 months would be:**

_____

_____

_____

6. **I am optimistic that I can and will achieve this.**

1	2	3	4	5	6	7	8	9	10

nope/not so much ○ ○ ○ ○ ○ ○ ○ ○ ○ yes!/I got this

Before we get clear on what's next, it is vital to understand where we are starting from. In other words, do we know what we want to accomplish? Do we feel heard, valued, and respected? Are we speaking up enough and to the right colleagues? This assessment will give you some clarity on where you are compared to where you'd like to be. Once you are done with this book and all of the exercises in it, I would like you to take this assessment again so you can see how far you've come!

Regardless of how you self-scored, I have good news and better news. There's a new level and hope for all of us. No one started out on top of their game. Even those who have achieved a high level of success doubt their ability and their worthiness or are fearful that they can't deliver, especially when there is a lot on the line.

Many times, our vision of what is possible rests on what we have experienced growing up or what the most influential people in our lives have achieved or not achieved. We are also deeply impacted by what our parents, teachers, early bosses, or other influential figures in our lives communicate to us. Did they make us feel less than, unworthy, incapable, or not good enough? Or did they champion our efforts and make us feel like we could achieve anything we put our minds to? These feelings from our past can be deeply imprinted on our belief system. We can be defined by others' opinions, by others' desire to keep us safe and therefore keep us small, or by others' fear that our succeeding will diminish or threaten their circumstances. Despite how you were raised, what you witnessed in yourself or in the women in your family, or if someone was a great believer in you or knowingly or unknowingly was kryptonite to your potential, you get to decide what you are capable of and the impact you will have on the world. Here's a story of a seemingly unlikely female leader who came from a simple beginning, who received the message growing up that she was unworthy yet went on to eventually have a meteoric rise at Microsoft.

From the Cornfields of Iowa to the Corner Office at Microsoft

Born into poverty, living in a one-bedroom home with her siblings and parents in rural Iowa, Jane Boulware overcame numerous challenges on her path to greatness. Early on, Jane received a message loud and clear that she was unworthy, that she didn't matter or was not good enough. Some of these messages were explicit, and some were implicit. Have you ever received a message that you were unworthy, either explicitly or implicitly? For me, the message came from my elementary school principal, Mrs. Harris, when she told me I was unworthy of remaining in my school. Despite working hard and receiving all As and Bs amid the chaos going on in my home growing up, those grades were not good enough. I was not good enough. I don't think Mrs. Harris used the exact word "unworthy," but that is the word that was emblazoned on my mind when I left her office in the fifth grade.

In Jane's case, it was her bucket story. As a child, Jane's accomplishments and memories were contained not in photo albums or scrapbooks but in a bucket that was kept in the attic of her small home in Iowa. One day the bucket that was marked "Jane" on the outside with a felt marker was tossed out by her parents. There went Jane's memories, special moments, and accomplishments, along with her feeling that these things mattered, that she mattered.

Even so, Jane was determined to get out of her small hometown in Iowa and not afraid or above doing what it took to gain experience and put some cash in her pocket. She began her working career as a carpet remnant salesperson, selling carpet scraps that her father gave her from his carpet installation business. Being from a small town where no one she knew was going on to higher education and lacking any encouragement or money from her parents made going to a university feel like a Herculean task or an unattainable dream.

Jane's resilience and persistence started young, and she did not allow anything to stand in her path to her own success. Eventually making it to college, Jane graduated as a forestry major. She then went on to attend graduate school and obtain an MBA. Shortly after, her climb up the corporate ladder began with a marketing role for Kimberly-Clark Corporation, where Jane spoke up, said yes when she didn't feel ready and asked for help often.

After many successful years, Jane was approached by Microsoft. Since Jane also had to consider her husband and her two children, making the decision to move to Washington was not an easy one.

Eventually, a joint decision was made, and once again, Jane said yes, this time to a corporate vice president of global marketing role. There were hiccups, challenges, and setbacks along the way, but Jane was not afraid to speak her mind and ask for what she wanted. Her courage and willingness to speak up eventually revealed an opportunity that was exciting but downright terrifying. Jane was asked to lead a team of all-male, non-English speaking employees from 16 countries in South America—a region known for machismo culture.

Jane thought it was a crazy idea. She had never worked outside of the country and didn't speak Spanish. But she trusted that her boss saw something in her that perhaps she didn't see in herself. You guessed it. Jane said yes, again. She bet on herself, and it paid off. Leading a global team in a foreign country did not come without challenges and second-guessing her decision, but ultimately, the experience and business outcome were wins for Jane, her international team, and for Microsoft.

You may or may not aspire to become a corporate executive, but the lesson from Jane's story is that worthiness stems from within. Jane decided she was worthy of a corner office, worthy of being a foreign, non-Spanish speaking woman leading the South American team, and worthy of being in the top 25 percent of leaders at Microsoft. Like Jane, we decide that we are worthy, and we choose ourselves. We decide what's possible and what we deserve.

Sometimes, we are unknowingly the barriers to our own success. As courageous as Jane was, for example, I'd be remiss if I didn't share that she had streaks of fear and doubt flash across her mind, especially when there were many unknowns, such as the case with her South American assignment. My hope for you is that you acknowledge your strengths and what you love to do, as well as listen for the whisper, or perhaps shout, that tells you to go for it.

Let's move forward to gain Clarity and create an Olympic-level runway so you can take flight to your next level of leadership. This is how you will look inside and determine your highest sense of integrity, your internal drivers, your why, and for whom you're fighting. For example, Jane decided she was not going to be poor. This was amplified when her sons were born. Jane also wanted to matter. She wanted out of her small town in Iowa, to have an impact. Based on how many rising leaders she's mentored and supported over the years, it seems as though Jane's North Star was to pave the way and make sure other female leaders felt seen and like they mattered.

Like Jane's experience early on in her career, Clarity can be vague at first. Once we begin to look inward and understand what drives our deepest desires, what makes us unique and valuable, it becomes easier to see what's next.

You may be wondering where to start. No need to lose one ounce of momentum. You begin by deciding you are ready. Deciding you do not need anyone else's permission. Deciding that you are more than good enough.
Are you ready?

If so, fantastic! We're ready to chart your path. If not, no problem. Stay with me. You'll get there. I promise!

Let's think about what's next for you in a different way. Imagine you are the captain of a ship. Let's say you decide to venture into uncharted territories, into open waters toward a magical island that your heart and gut have been pulling you toward. You likely know the nearby continent and the vicinity of the island, but you do not know the exact island or which part of it is best to approach. Whether you arrive or not is left to chance. It will be uncertain if you'll arrive at all. If you do arrive, the journey will certainly take longer than if you had a

SHERYL KLINE, M.A. CHPC

road map. Having confidence in your ability is vital, as is having influence over your crew. But first, you need to know specifically where you're going. You need to chart your path and know how to manage course corrections. I invite you to become the captain of your ship and learn how to chart your path.

SECTION 1

Clarity:
Chart Your Path

"The only limit to our realization of tomorrow

will be our doubts of today."

— *Franklin D. Roosevelt*

Many times, lacking clarity paralyzes us. We ask, "What's next for me?" but we don't know the answer, how to get there, or even what's possible. The good news is that this is 100 percent normal. Having purpose- driven clarity can be elusive and fluid. It changes as we have different experiences and learn from others. The not-so-good news is that a lack of clarity can keep us stuck. Clarity is key because it will give you the outside lines of the sketch you'll fill in as you take action. Every action is valuable, even the mistakes or the actions that feel like mistakes. More accurately, it's the mistakes and setbacks that can be our greatest guides toward what's next. Here's a good place to pause and have a little more grace with yourself. Pay tribute and have gratitude for the mountains you have already climbed as well as the things that are perceived as failures or setbacks. From here, know you did your best at the time and reflect on the lessons learned.

Reflection:

What is something that you've accomplished that you're proud of? What's an example of something that you did or something that happened to you that you could consider with a little more grace? What lesson(s) did you learn?

_____

_____

_____

Are you ready to start filling in the lines of your current or next masterpiece? I'm excited to light up the way. You may be surprised, though, that your journey forward is not about you. World-class performers know how to tap into a power greater than themselves to gain motivation, inspiration, and courage. When the journey feels difficult, improbable, or impossible, they have a reserve of strength and guidance to pull from. Let's make that available to you too.

Imagine you're in an airplane headed for a fabulous, faraway destination that you've always dreamed of visiting. The pilot, however, is unclear on the exact path and has the nose of the airplane off by 1 percent. As you take off, this slight miscalculation is insignificant. Hours into the flight, when you're about to land, you hear the flight attendant announce that you're arriving at a destination that's hundreds of miles from where you intended.

There is an aviation principle to aid pilots in navigation called the 1 in 60 Rule. Essentially, after each 60 nautical miles, one degree of error in heading will result in being off course by one nautical mile. So, just being slightly off course at the beginning of a journey will result in becoming further off course the longer you travel.

What about when we feel off course in our career journey, in our current role, in a project we're working on, in how we feel our voice is heard, in our current industry, or in the impact we feel we're having (or not having)? How long do we go on, and how far do we veer off course until there is a significant impact on productivity, profitability, innovative ability, impact, and most importantly, joy?

While there's no steadfast calculation like the 1 in 60 Rule for the consequences of not having world- class clarity on your highest sense of purpose and contribution, would it be unreasonable that the cost to your joy, ability to sustain your success, and your company's bottom line could be building significantly over time?

Clarity is key for organizations to course correct before getting too far off course by losing top female talent and failing to retain them in their pipeline. For emerging leaders, you are only limited by what you cannot see. If you know you are off course, but feel the pain, time, or discomfort of course correcting is too much, I got you. We'll be covering a proven process that can help you become crystal clear on what matters most to you, why you care so deeply about it, and how to envision your most important moments materializing.

Have you ever felt like you had something more or something different to give? Maybe it's time to shift or pivot. Maybe you were being called for more or to step outside your comfort zone. Did you disregard these nudges or find yourself pulling back?

I did for decades. The "not good enough" message was so ingrained in my belief of who I was that it was like there was a bully standing in front of me with his arms crossed, denying me a way forward or even a start. I allowed this bully in my mind to dim and almost extinguish my light until I decided I was good enough.

You get to decide, too.

SHERYL KLINE, M.A. CHPC

CHAPTER 2

Integrity

'Slow time and listen to your gut and intuition.'

-Sheryl Kline

What's next for you or your next level of impact does not start with what you want to achieve or a goal you have in mind. It's all too common to decide on concrete goals with little or no regard for the aspirations, guidance, and consulting of our souls. It's our soul that knows our highest sense of integrity, what's most important for us to be congruent and happy, which is when we can do our best work. It also lets us know when it's time to go or when something or someone is a hard no. Understanding your highest sense of integrity is your North Star that lights up your unique path and dims the wrong ones.

If you're aware, paying attention, and willing to listen, that is.

SHERYL KLINE, M.A. CHPC

What moral principles guide and define you and make you feel congruent with your soul?

_____

_____

_____

What are you doing now that makes your soul sing, that makes you smile and proud?

_____

_____

_____

If you were to choose three words that define the best version of yourself or the person you aspire to be, which words come to mind?

_____

_____

_____

If these questions are giving you a headache or making you even more frustrated, what's next for you is to schedule "white space" in your calendar where you are unplugged (e.g., no podcasts, phone calls, notifications—ideally no phone) and can be in nature and alone. If you choose to spend this time with someone else, I recommend it being in silence. Be present with your surroundings, observe what you see and think, and surrender to your thoughts without judgment. If you're wondering how long and/or how often these walks or times in nature should be, consistency is most important. Give yourself a range of time and a number of days. For example, five to 10 minutes three to four days a week. Once you begin doing this, be sure to have a dedicated journal to capture the sights, sounds, and thoughts you experience when you get back.

According to a New York Times article, The Beauty of a Silent Walk, "Walking in silence is an ancient tradition rooted in mindfulness, a form of meditation that helps people focus on the physical sensations, thoughts, and emotions of the present moment, without any judgment."

Whether this sounds like a dreamy opportunity or a torturous waste of time, consider the epic smash hit Hamilton. According to Inc. Magazine, "The creator of the Tony-, Grammy-, and Pulitzer Prize-winning musical came up with the idea for the show while he was chilling on a lounge chair in Mexico."

"When I picked up Ron Chernow's biography [of Alexander Hamilton], I was at a resort in Mexico on my first vacation from In the Heights, which I had been working seven years to bring to Broadway," Lin-Manuel Miranda once told entrepreneur and author Ariana Huffington in an interview. "The moment my brain got a moment's rest, Hamilton walked into it."

He added, "It's no accident that the best idea I've ever had in my life—perhaps maybe the best one I'll ever have in my life—came to me on vacation."

Whether you're aspiring to write and star in one of the most successful plays on Broadway, or you're looking to speak up more, ask for what you're worth, or make a shift, create the environment where your soul can speak to you.

Integrity is a holistic concept that comes from within. Regardless of the environment we are in (work, family, community, or in public), world-class performers strive to show up as the best versions of themselves and course, correct with humility, compassion, and grace. To feel the joy associated with being on this trajectory, we must be clear about who we are how we want to show up in the world and give ourselves the gift of calm and joy.

Reflection: Can this be on the same page as the question and lines below?

What are your three words?

_____

_____

_____

How and when will you block out time to relax and be calm in an environment that brings you joy?

_____

_____

_____

Coaching Illustration:

Over the course of her more than 25-year uber successful sales career, Angie (not her real name) felt like she had to work longer, harder, and push the limits of what she felt in her gut and in her heart was right. She sometimes felt herself compromising her integrity to meet the demands of her CEO, who in turn had demands from his board. As her career took off, she often heard, "I don't care how you do it. Just make it happen," when referring to quarterly sales goals. She made it happen, but the whisper from her soul said, "This isn't right, and I'll never be in this position or compromise my integrity to 'reach a number' again."

Unfortunately, Angie was put in a similar position again, now with a different company. The post-COVID boom was over, the supply chain was not the biggest problem, the sales leaders and their teams had to roll up their sleeves and sell again, and the demands on her region were closing in.

There was a time when Angie would have no time to herself due to domestic and international calls at all hours, constantly traveling even when feeling unwell, and enduring the emotional and physical toll that came along with being "on" too often and not speaking up for what she knew was right. Angie knew it was time for a shift, but she was just too busy or tired to access the wisdom that held the answers for her.

Part of the coaching process that I led Angie through in order to regain clarity was to set a couple of key boundaries and reset her priorities, making her well-being a priority. The boundaries involved shutting off devices, limiting how and when she could be contacted, and regaining control of her calendar. For example, the first hour of Angie's day was hers. She took a few moments to journal, drink a glass of water, take a short walk with her dog at sunrise, and organize her day. This involved either waking up earlier or taking this "first hour" after the occasional four o'clock in the morning global leadership meeting with her European peers and CEO. Angie also shut down all work devices and turned off notifications between six and seven o'clock every night to be with her family, and her phone became off-limits to colleagues for work requests or questions.

What's next did not become clear until Angie created white space for herself, which allowed her to hear her internal voice. Using three words— transparent, confident, and authentic—as her guiding principles, she asked herself, "What about my role is congruent with my values? Where is my 'line in the sand' for what will be asked of me? Do I have the support of my leadership or is there an opportunity to push important projects and initiatives through to have a bigger voice?" Most importantly, Angie asked herself if she could stay true to her highest sense of integrity. Could she be transparent, confident, and authentic?

Gaining clarity of her highest sense of integrity helped Angie understand that a change needed to be made and uncovered a big decision she would soon make.

As fate would have it, her next monthly 15- minute one-on-one with her boss also included the company's chief human resources officer. After building world-class and high-performing teams, forming irreplaceable relationships with some of her company's biggest and most lucrative customers, and driving unprecedented growth through the duration of the COVID-19 pandemic, Angie was let go.

Gaining clarity about "what's next" in her role shifted to gaining clarity on the best exit package she could negotiate. There was a gap between the figure that Angie wanted and what she was comfortable asking for. Angie was clear on the amount of time she wanted to take a pause and then find the right next role, but funding that pause was going to require a big ask.

What exactly was this big ask going to be? What was Angie's gut and heart telling her that she needed and that she was worth? Those were important questions. In the process of building world-class clarity, we start with the end in mind: very high level and aspirational, vague, maybe even a little foggy at first. Refining clarity is like painting a masterpiece. Sketch the outside lines, step back, see how it looks and feels, and envision how the painting looks and how you'll feel once it's finished and exceeds your expectations.

For Angie, we worked on filling in her lines by taking a three-week sabbatical in the summer so she could disconnect, focus on herself, and take time to rest. She spent time in nature, journaling, and slowing down with friends, family, and alone time. When Angie returned, she was ready to follow the process and determine what was next.

Here are a few of the questions that Angie answered that helped her get out of the whirlwind in her mind and get ready to create a new plan:

1. What would make me feel happy and proud in my current role/future role?

_____

_____

_____

2. What makes me uncomfortable or feel incongruent in my role?

_____

_____

_____

3. What's most important to me to become more congruent with the highest version of myself?

_____

_____

_____

CHAPTER 3

Legacy Builder:
Getting Clear on Your Future Legacy
Today

"Stick to your true north.

Build greatness for the long-term."

— *Ruth Porat, former CFO, Alphabet*

Are you familiar with the parable about the three bricklayers? After the Great Fire of London in 1666 that leveled the city, the world's most famous architect at the time, Christopher Wren, was commissioned to rebuild St Paul's Cathedral.

According to Jim Baker in his book Sacred Structures, "One day in 1671, Christopher Wren observed three bricklayers on a scaffold, one crouched, one half-standing and one standing tall, working very hard and fast. To the first bricklayer, Christopher Wren asked the question, 'What are you doing?' to which the bricklayer replied, 'I'm a bricklayer.

I'm working hard, laying bricks to feed my family.' The second bricklayer responded, 'I'm a builder. I'm building a wall.' But the third bricklayer, the most productive of the three and the future leader of the group, when asked the question, 'What are you doing?' replied with a gleam in his eye. 'I'm a cathedral builder. I'm building a great cathedral to the Almighty.'"

When it comes to your legacy and how you'd like to be remembered, what is deeply important to you? More importantly, how do you assign importance to it? For example, a client and marketing leader for a tech company is on the board for a women-in tech organization. For Shannon (not her real name), it's not about getting and keeping more women in tech. What speaks to her is changing the current environment for women in tech and shifting the institution so that it's a better and more welcoming environment for women. Much like the third bricklayer, Shannon assigned a higher purpose to her endeavor. Shannon is helping to shift an industry that is rapidly changing the world and making it safer for her daughters. Like the third bricklayer, Shannon is "building a cathedral to the Almighty" because her legacy is rooted in what's most dear to her.

Throughout history, courageous people have crafted legacies that defy what's possible, legacies born from a fierce refusal to accept the injustices of their times. Rosa Parks, for example, is a testament to this truth. A seamstress in Montgomery, Alabama, she wasn't seeking fame, nor was she the first to resist segregation. Yet on a December evening in 1955, with a clarity that comes from profound weariness of spirit, she took a standby, remaining seated on a segregated bus. In her autobiography, My Story, she recounts this pivotal moment, not with a description of physical exhaustion but with a declaration of being "tired of giving in."

Her quiet defiance ignited a revolution, a blaze that swept through the nation, changing the Civil Rights Movement and altering the course of history. Rosa Parks' investment in a future of equity and justice was her legacy—a legacy that transcended her life and continues to inspire.

This is the challenge before you: Mark an inflection point in history that served as a springboard for women and those in the margins. Reflect on the imprints you leave—how is your company different because of your presence? Whose journeys have you made easier?

Your legacy, though it bears your signature, isn't just about you. It's about the lives you touch and transform. It's about the difference you make when you step into or out of a role, transition to a new opportunity, or simply conclude a meeting. Consider the ways in which others are changed because of your presence, how you inspire, and how that inspiration takes root and grows.

With clarity and conviction, you have the power to shape your future—to inspire your team, to mold the culture within your company, and to pave the way for the women who will follow you. There's a ripple effect when we lock arms in solidarity, committing to forge a better world by living into our legacies today.

Who's Your Who?

You may be familiar with the importance of knowing your "why." In other words, why do you care so deeply about the industry you are in, the promotion you want and deserve, or the bigger voice you'd like to have with your leadership? Something that is not spoken about as widely is the importance of knowing your "who."

In two decades of research and work with world-class athletes and Olympians, I learned that they are rarely competing just for themselves. They are running for a person or running for a cause. In the case of a track and field Olympic gold medalist, Leroy Dixon, he was running to save his family. In high school he noticed that his parents were arguing all the time, and his sisters were not doing well in their endeavors.

When he was noticed by the track coach while playing on the basketball team in high school, he initially declined the invitation to join the track team. The track coach was persistent, though, so Leroy finally gave in. Consequently, he quickly rose to the top ranks of track and field, eventually winning gold and silver medals at the Olympics. What made this novice Olympian defeat the odds against much more seasoned athletes who were taller and more muscular? It was his "who," his family. He noticed that the faster he ran, the happier his parents seemed, and his sisters were inspired to work harder at their endeavors. Leroy Dixon told me that he was running to save his family. His "who" was more important to him than the worry or doubt that came along with standing next to bigger and more decorated track stars.

For me, the purpose is deeply personal. I am driven by the memory of my mother, Barbara. Her voice went unheard, her sense of purpose unfulfilled, and her ability to be a conservationist unrealized. I gained my sense of purpose and courage from my mother because I'm passionate about the importance of her voice and the impact it could have had in our home and for the owls that she was so passionate about saving. Whether speaking at a national conference, coaching executive female leaders, or their teams, my purpose is clear—

to equip women with the tools to amplify their voices so that collectively, women can return to power and h e l p c o u r s e correct our companies and our communities toward profitability, productivity, and peace.

Reflect on a person, past or present, who sparked something within you. How did they inspire you? Draw strength from their example. Contemplate how you wish to be remembered, and let that vision guide you. This could be an immediate family member(s), friend, daughter, niece, or even a figure in history.

Reflection:

Who is this person for you, and what is it about him or her that inspires you?

_____

_____

_____

I believe wholeheartedly that we are only limited by what we think is possible, and we gain strength and courage from important figures in o u r lives. To craft a legacy that reflects your highest aspirations, you must trust your intuition—that sacred place where heart and gut meet.

This could manifest in something as straightforward as

being purposeful in your next conversation or as grand as pursuing a bold, audacious dream. Determine how you want to be remembered, both in the immediate and long term and start embodying that legacy now.

Your legacy is a canvas waiting for you to decide what colors to use and how to fill it in. It is not for others to judge whether you are capable or worthy of creating it. From the memory you leave behind in a meeting to the mark you make across your career, it's in your hands to seize opportunities, to speak out, to be present—through triumphs and setbacks. Each decision you make is part of your legacy and has the potential to inspire many.

Legacy is not just the story of where you've been. It's the blueprint of the impact you'll continue to make. It's the values you instill, the standards you uphold, and the examples you set. It's the courage to make the difficult choices and the wisdom to celebrate the victories, however small. It's the resilience to push forward when faced with adversity and the humility to step back and lift others into the spotlight.

Now, try answering these questions. Think about what you're passionate about, what you are good at, and what you'd like to learn. Assign a deeper meaning to what you aspire to do, and imagine it's already happened.

1. What legacy did I create? / How am I remembered?

_____

_____

_____

2. Why did I matter?

_____

_____

_____

3. What did I contribute to, and whose lives did I impact?

_____

_____

_____

You've completed the hardest part of becoming an even greater Fearless Female Leader: Looking with curious eyes deep into your past, envisioning your future, and consulting your heart about your highest sense of integrity and what's most important in your character. Now, you're ready to roll up your sleeves and chart your path! Let's build a world- class Success Roadmap™ so you can get crystal clear on what's next and how to get there.

C H A P T E R 4

Success Roadmap™:
A Blueprint to What's Next

"I always did something I was a little not ready to do.
I think that's how you grow. When there's that moment of
'Wow, I'm not really sure I can do this,' and you push
through those moments, that's when you have a
breakthrough."
— *Marissa Mayer Former CEO, Yahoo!*

After working with dozens of female executives over the years, as well as other world-class performers in athletics, I've learned that we sometimes tell ourselves stories that are rarely, if ever, accurate. When we hear whispers that tell us we are not good enough, not ready, not worthy, or that we are an imposter, they are voices or experiences from our past that are trying to shape our future. More often than not, the stories could not be further from the truth. Remember Jane? No money, no support from her parents, no connections, no clear path to college until she created one, and no confidence that she'd ever be one of 150 executives in a company of 60,000 and be responsible for billions of dollars in revenue. Jane's path could have been very different if she kept telling herself that story instead of attending college and graduate school and saying yes to various assignments that she was not ready for at Kimberly Clark and eventually at Microsoft. Like Jane, you get to chart your path to where you want to go, regardless of your current or past circumstances.

The journey toward achieving a dream— whether it's reaching a certain level of executive leadership, spearheading transformative initiatives, or launching a bold enterprise—can be like a voyage across an uncharted sea. The destination may seem like a fuzzy silhouette against the horizon, daunting in its distance and scale.

History tells us that human potential is limitless. History's most accomplished women suggest a reassuring truth: The sense of impossibility is a common prelude to extraordinary achievement. If you're wrestling with doubts, take comfort in knowing that this path is well-trodden by the courageous, bias- busting, stereotype-breaking women who now light your way. To believe you are capable and worthy of the impossible requires a mindset shift paired with a proven world-class strategy. Tools to build Olympic-level confidence combined with a well-conceived plan can offer a shield against the unwanted visitors of doubt, imposter syndrome, and disabling fear. Oprah Winfrey's assertion that "Luck is a matter of preparation meeting opportunity. Planning is key to success" is the truth. It's a testament to the power of designing what you desire and seeing it come to life.

Does this process guarantee your success? Not exactly. There are many variables at play; some are in your control, and some are not. What creating a Success Roadmap™ will do is help to give you your best shot at surrendering to what's possible for you and staying the course to what you have control over.

The result?

You'll either get there or you'll have tried your best and discovered new opportunities that would have otherwise never existed.

World-class performers, whether leaders in their field or Olympians, all share a commonality: They begin with the end in mind, with a vision of triumph as a preordained destiny. Their success is reverse engineered as if it's already happened. This process of reverse engineering success forces us to become problem solvers rather than a doubter. If we lose, fail, or don't get the raise, the job, or the promotion, there must be another way. There must be because the finish line has already happened, so we must have taken a wrong turn. It's not that we weren't meant to run the race. We have grace, humility, and self-compassion for trying. Dust off and keep going. You, too, can adopt this approach. Envision your success as a present reality.

I am/I've achieved:

_____

_____

_____

It makes me feel:

_____

_____

_____

One example of the impact that I'm having is:

_____

_____

_____

Others who benefit from this impact are:

_____

_____

_____

They are impacted in this way:

_____

_____

_____

If you truly believed that a future desire has already happened, how would such an achievement alter what you are doing now? What new skills would you hone? What would you say yes to? What relationships would you form or deepen? While no strategy guarantees success, as life's certainties are few, this method of envisioning and planning will propel you toward your aspirations with clarity and a new sense of urgency.

The practice of reverse engineering a goal may be familiar to you, yet within goal setting is an Olympic-level secret often overlooked: For goals to be as successful and likely as possible, there must be different goals for different periods of time. There are long-term objectives, intermediate-term objectives, and short-term objectives, each with their own guidelines for successful completion. Without knowing this and planning accordingly, we set ourselves up for frustration and failure and pose a strong temptation for us to lose fortitude.

Long-Term Objectives

Your Success Roadmap™ begins with the end in mind, with your long-term objective, a lofty stretch goal that's typically at least six months to a year away. A goal that often feels out of our control. If your long- term objective makes you a little uncomfortable, that's good! If you have complete control over a long-term goal, it's likely that you're not pushing yourself to your potential. You'll know if your long-term objective is right for you if you feel a sense of excitement along with a twinge or jolt of nervousness.

For example, Sue (not her real name) is a channel sales director. In 10 years, she envisions being a channel chief at a technology company. Her long- term objective is to do her first keynote at a major industry conference and be promoted to the VP level within one year. For Sue, the nervousness that came with this goal was less like a twinge and more like a jolt that almost sidelined her. As Sue made peace with her emotions around what her heart and gut were telling her to go for, she learned to become an observer and not a judge.

Sue made peace with the fact that she had almost no control over whether she'd ever become a channel chief at a technology company, no control over what opportunities would be available, and no control over the competition.

Sue's vision of becoming a channel chief was like receiving a wrapped birthday gift in January that couldn't be opened until a summer birthday. A gift that she knew existed, had a bow around it, and that she put on her closet shelf until her big day. She could see it and believed it was there. It was just a matter of time before she got to open it.

Long-term objectives are similar. Proceed as if it's already happened and success is inevitable. Focus on the process, detach from the outcome, and trust that the journey will steer you in the right direction even when it feels uncomfortable, uncertain, or improbable.

What about you?

What do you dream of becoming, doing, or achieving? What is something that makes you feel excited but a little bit apprehensive? Remember, long- term objectives are not SMART goals that we often hear about. They are not specific, measurable, achievable, relevant, or time-based. You do not have control or even certainty that it can or will happen. Your long- term objective just needs to be a stretch goal that lights you up inside and one that's remotely possible in the next six months to a year.

For example, Sue's long-term objective to be promoted to sales director in a year as an important stepping stone to channel chief is a stretch in her current organization, where there's lots of competition and no guarantees she'll get there. Sue does not have control over this promotion. Instead, she does have faith that not only will it happen, but that it's already happened. This mindset helps Sue stay motivated, keep doubt at bay, and show up every day as the leader she'd like to become.

Let's Chart Your Path!

My Fearless Female Leadership long-term objective is (little to no control, at least a little audacious, at least remotely possible):

_____

_____

_____

Amazing! Take a pause, put your hand on your heart, and honor yourself, perhaps for dreaming a little bigger and giving yourself permission to listen to what your heart and gut are calling you toward. You are the only one required to grant permission to decide if you're good enough, worthy, or capable.

Take a bow! You are learning how the top 1 percent think, beginning with the end in mind. You are learning to lean into one of my favorite quotes: "Proceed as if success is inevitable. One day, you'll be called, and you'll be ready."

You are world-class. You are dreaming big and beginning with the end in mind. Now it is time to prepare for the next step in the journey, to have an honest assessment of how proficient our current self really is. Let's move from accepting what is outside our control to reverse engineering our next level of leadership and contribution.

Intermediate-Term Objectives

Here's where your Success Roadmap™ starts to take shape, where you get to start taking control and filling in the lines with what you desire. Your intermediate-term objectives are within reach, where you'll focus on what's most important for you to improve over the next couple of weeks to the next couple of months. For those of you who like to have control (me included!), here is where you can make important decisions and begin to take tangible steps to close a gap that may feel a little unwieldy at first. Here is where you will focus on the process of improving, show up as the leader you aspire to become, and have faith that this vulnerability and commitment will lead you to where you want to go.

Intermediate-term objectives are quantifiable goals that require you to take an honest look at yourself, your capabilities, and your proficiencies as your present-day self as opposed to your future self, who has already achieved your long-term objective. For example, picture yourself six months into achieving your vision of a promotion or a new role, living in the reality you once only hoped for. To identify the intermediate-term objectives that will get you there, ask yourself: What skills are different between my current and future self? What are my knowledge gaps? These questions will help you arrive at the quantifiable steps you'll methodically chip away at as you move toward your long-term objective and the leader you aspire to be.

Let the answers to the above questions guide you toward what to take action on now. List them— make them specific, actionable, and measurable. Whether it's mastering public speaking, honing your negotiation skills, or deepening key relationships, each goal should be clear and measurable. For example, "I sign up for a public speaking class on LinkedIn and join Toastmasters to practice weekly."

What new competencies do you have?

_____

_____

_____

Which ones have you sharpened?

_____

_____

_____

What's one way you will take action to improve?

_____

_____

_____

For Sue to gain visibility on her journey to being a director and eventually becoming a channel chief, it was her public speaking skills that needed improving. She knew speaking internally at leadership meetings as well as being a keynote speaker at conferences was important. There were two challenges for Sue. She was petrified of public speaking, and she had never spoken at a conference, let alone delivered a keynote. She had also never asked to attend or present at senior leadership meetings. When Sue rated herself on a scale of 1 to 10 for speaking, she gave herself a 2. To meet her long-term objective of becoming one who spoke at conferences and internal leadership meetings, Sue decided she needed to be at least at a 7.

When I asked Sue what else a channel director embodied that she was yet to master, without a pause, she said, "Knowledge of the business and developing a tracking and accountability process for herself and her team." I argued that Sue's response seemed like two separate proficiencies. She was adamant and excited to take these on, so we made these collectively her second intermediate-term objective. At that time, Sue rated herself as a 4 out of 10 on these objectives. Where would she need to be as a director of channel sales? She said at least an 8.

How about YOU?

Let's chart your path!

My intermediate-term objective #1 is: (quantifiable/measurable, vital to improve to achieve my LTO)

_____

_____

_____

My intermediate-term objective #2 is:

_____

_____

_____

Raising your hand and being willing to learn and grow means that you are already world-class! Olympic athletes who have been at the top of their game like Simone Biles, Serena Williams, Kobe Bryant, or Roger Federer, to name a few, never feel like they are done learning or don't need to improve. The same goes for the most respected and influential female executives that I've had the honor of working with. They were aware and grateful for what they achieved, but there was always a next level to reach or room for improvement. You have already achieved success and had an impact. Your willingness to learn and improve are the same qualities of those who have achieved the impossible. Take that in for a moment. Now, you might be wondering about the most important things you can do to fill the gaps for your long-term objectives.

Short-Term Objectives

As we look ahead to lofty goals and initiatives, what

inspires world-class performers to stay motivated when the road gets difficult when there are setbacks and failures? It's having control over the process, over the sometimes small yet vital steps toward improving. Your short-term objectives are part of your Success Roadmap™ that keeps you grounded, motivated, and feeling like you have some control over what you would like to accomplish.

Short-term objectives answer the question, "What can I do consistently to become more proficient in my intermediate-term objectives so I can make measurable progress toward reaching my long-term objectives?" Inspiration and motivation come from hunkering down and focusing on the most controllable steps toward making progress in the direction you want to go. If you've ever been to a baseball game, you can imagine short-term objectives are like the small steps you take walking from the baseball diamond to the nosebleed seats at the top of the stadium. Even though it's a long way, if you keep taking steps methodically and consistently, you eventually make it to the top.

Resistance: The Little Devil That Does Not Want You to Succeed

Let's be honest. Your road may be challenging, and your journey may sometimes feel futile. This is called resistance (Singer 2007). Resistance is like a scared animal that lashes out so that anyone approaching will stop in their tracks. Resistance feeds on fear, doubt, worry, and unworthiness. Resistance is the voice that tries to keep us safe by protecting our egos and enticing us to play small. Resistance points its finger at you and says, "You're an imposter. You are not good enough. You don't check enough boxes. You should give up." Resistance is a squirrely, scared, and stubborn voice that is fueled by our negative experiences with others, by harsh words we heard, or by cruel actions we witnessed during our formidable years.

Short-term objectives keep resistance at bay because you have control over them. The steps you decide to take defuse resistance and lessen its power. Eventually, the resistance you feel can be transformed into rocket fuel for your success—something you'll learn in the Confidence chapter. For now, let's continue charting our path, learning to stay motivated, and making progress despite any resistance that may pay us a visit.

Unlike long-term and intermediate-term objectives, short-term objectives are entirely under your command. You have complete control. They are the commitments that will, brick by brick, build the road to your dreams—if only you lay them with consistency, with focus, and with care.

Are your short-term objectives a guarantee that you will achieve your long-term objective? According to my dad, "Only two things in life are guaranteed: death and taxes." No, short-term objectives do not guarantee you'll succeed, but they will give you your best shot.

As we dive deeper into your Success Roadmap™, let's foster the commitment to stay as productive and motivated as possible. Your Success Roadmap™ does this by outlining different near-term goals as well as ones that are far off in the distant. Without understanding how our perception of time impacts goal setting, we set ourselves up for potential setbacks, burnout, or wanting to quit altogether. With a couple of world-class tools in your goal-setting tool belt, you'll be able to maneuver these sometimes common but avoidable pitfalls. (Neason 2013).

Understanding the power of how to plan and achieve incremental progress is crucial. Each small step may not seem significant on its own, but collectively, they can accumulate and gain power. Like a powerful river that begins as a trickle of water, short-term objectives accumulate and are vital parts of your long- term objective puzzle. Keep chipping away, and a floodgate of opportunity is possible.

Let's determine the controllable acts of courage and small decisions that can help you make progress toward where you'd like to be. Breaking down the seemingly overwhelming into manageable tasks and celebrating the incremental victories that pave the way to larger successes are what will keep you moving forward.

For example, Sue decided that the actionable and controllable short-term objectives she could take to become a keynote speaker and learn the finance intricacies of her business would be most important. Sue blocked out time to take a public speaking class on LinkedIn and committed to practicing after each class. Despite being nervous, she asked to speak at an upcoming meeting with her boss and colleagues, knowing it would be important for her visibility. She also met with her controller multiple times in an effort to better understand business finance.

The specificity of these commitments helped Sue stay accountable to herself and improve the things that her future leader self would need to be proficient in. She focused by turning off the notifications on her phone and computer, letting her family and colleagues know that she was unavailable, and outlining, researching, and presenting her findings. For accountability (which we'll discuss more in later chapters), Sue messaged a colleague when her daily short-term objectives were complete.

Let's Chart Your Path!

My short-term objectives are:

_____

_____

_____

While the Success Roadmap™ is an individualized guide for you to create and follow, it is important to remain flexible. Just as a sailor must adjust their course in response to weather changes, you must adapt plans in response to life's ever-changing circumstances. This flexibility, paired with a commitment to your long-term objective, is the bedrock of a resilient and successful strategy.

For example, Jane, the Microsoft executive, never planned to lead a team in South America. When she accepted the opportunity, her short- and intermediate-term objectives changed almost overnight. She had to learn a new business and a new language while making personal adjustments for her family. Remember, have a plan and focus on the process, but be flexible if an opportunity presents itself that you decide is right for you.

Your Success Roadmap™ emphasizes the importance of self-awareness and reflection. Success is as much about internal alignment as it is about external achievements. Understanding your motivations, recognizing your strengths, and acknowledging areas for growth are all critical components of your success plan.

In charting your path, acknowledge that success is a process without a final destination. It involves a series of choices, actions, and evaluations. Set milestones that not only guide you but also motivate and inspire you. These milestones will serve as checkpoints, moments to pause, reflect, and celebrate how far you've come.

As you put a stake in the ground and take consistent action, remember that your Success Roadmap™ is unique to you. It reflects your ambitions, values, and the impact you wish to make. It is both a guide and a testament to your commitment to achieving greatness for yourself and for others.

Let this roadmap be your guide, your motivator, and your reminder that the road to success is paved with intention, action, and the belief that anything is possible. With every step you take, you are not only moving closer to your goals but also becoming open to and shaping the person you are destined to be.

During various inflection points on our journey to achieve our long-term objective, we will encounter moments that could change everything, that could accelerate or decelerate our journey. If you were an Olympian, you'd prepare for those moments 10 times more than you thought necessary. World-class performers never leave important moments to chance. What's next for you is your Olympics. Let's make sure you are prepared so when you're called to show up and speak up, you'll be ready.

SHERYL KLINE, M.A. CHPC

C H A P T E R 5

Moments

"We must believe that we are gifted for something
and that this thing, at whatever cost,
must be attained."

— *Marie Curie*

Have you ever catastrophized an upcoming conversation or event? One where you'll be making a big ask or one that reminds you of a time you were denied or shut down previously? Perhaps you have an exciting interview coming up, but it's coming after 74 other interviews that have not panned out. Maybe you'll be asking your boss for a raise, promotion, or to be involved in a project that you have little experience in. Based on the research in the Harvard Business Review, if you catastrophize, it means you're human and not alone. "Catastrophizing is a common reaction to uncertain situations where we tend to overestimate the likelihood or consequences of our worst fears," writes Meg Jay in *What*

To Do When Your Mind (always) Focuses on the Worst-Case Scenario.

A very large World Economic Forum mental health study says this could be especially relevant for those under the age of 35. Until then, the part of our brain that deals with uncertainties is still developing. Without the tools to manage the real fear we experience about the past or future, this type of catastrophizing can spike emotion, therefore disabling the ability to make decisions, stay productive, take calculated risks, innovate, and stay motivated.

Not long ago I had the pleasure of speaking with a brilliant 30-year-old woman who clearly had an impressive education, work ethic, and trailblazing contribution in her six years in channel sales. Kim (not her real name) was eventually swept into one of the various waves of tech layoffs in 2023. Based on her track record, many recommendations, connections, and sheer optimism and determination, Kim was confident that she'd land a new role in three months. When three months turned into six, then nine, Kim understandably found it challenging not to catastrophize whenever she made it to round two, three, or four of her interviews.

As you'll learn more later, what we think is portrayed through our tone, gestures, and body language. When we catastrophize, the movie reel in our mind can keep going until we end up somewhere unfamiliar and upsetting. We assume another rejection is coming, that we'll never find a new role, fall behind on our bills, have to take in a roommate to pay our rent or mortgage, maybe move somewhere cheaper, lose our friends, be thought of as a loser by our family and friends, and end up penniless and lonely. This may be a little dramatic, but you get the idea. If this runaway train in our mind is not back on the tracks during our important interactions, we're setting ourselves up for a crash.

When my daughter was in middle school, she catastrophized about what might happen if she received a poor grade on a math quiz that she did not feel prepared for. In between sobs and gasps for breath one afternoon, she said, "The grade on the quiz will mean I might do poorly on my next test, which is 30 percent of my grade. If I tank that test, I might not pass the class. If I don't pass the class, I will not be able to get into the best math class in my first year in high school, which means that my college options will be limited or non-existent. I'll have no college education and end up living under a bridge." Until she learned to manage her emotions and ability to stay present when under pressure, doing well on exams was challenging.

I'm happy to say my daughter is a college graduate with a great job, but this is a dramatic yet real example of how our minds can pick up steam and run toward the negative. We're genetically wired to fear uncertainty. According to the Mental Health Foundation in the UK, "Early man would have feared attack by predators, famine, disease, and disputes with other communities. Fear would have played a key part in human evolution, as many biologists and anthropologists have attested." Therefore, it makes sense that the most primitive parts of our brains tend to take a "better safe than sorry" approach to uncertainty whether we face a small threat such as being reprimanded by our boss, or a larger threat such as losing our job.

From an evolutionary standpoint. if there is a sabertoothed tiger lurking around the corner and I'm not careful, I could be eaten. That type of catastrophizing can save our lives. We require tools, though, to manage this evolutionary protection mechanism or to use it to our advantage. Otherwise, we could be lured out of the present by perceived threats, which can make our best performance inaccessible.

I'm not sure about you, but I'm a planner for my business, travel, and social get-togethers. I love predictability, certainty, and control, maybe because it was missing at a formidable time in my life. My instincts for safety, protection, and predictability are strong. In certain circumstances, these drivers can be helpful, even necessary, but at other times, they can prevent me from taking necessary risks. So, it's important to learn when to challenge these tendencies. There is power in realizing when our instincts and emotions keep us safe and when they box us in.

In day-to-day life, uncertainties can be like smoke. Our job is to figure out whether a problem, setback, or concern is more like burnt toast, a house fire, or just a false alarm and respond accordingly. Even though it's rarely easy, let's begin the process of rewiring and harnessing your instincts so they work to your advantage.

When creating a Success Roadmap™ for your long-term objective, it's important to think through how you would like a situation to turn out and then reverse engineer how you can prepare to make that happen. In preparing for the moments that matter, you are like an Olympian levelling up her training. It's the small yet consistent and important things that no one else sees or rewards you for that will accelerate your progress.

For example, if you're looking to gain buy-in from your boss on a major request, start by envisioning a yes from your boss and work backward from there. How will you make your case, provide data and facts to back your request, and prove that your request is a good idea for you, your boss, and the company? Visualizing your end goal is a great place to start, but it's an incomplete plan and can derail your effort if your boss says no.

Kim, for example, eventually landed a role she was proud of and excited about. Yet, just barely after her three-month mark, when an important moment came with her boss—the crucial meeting that could have been an important steppingstone to her dream role—she stumbled. The preparation strategies she had in place and the hopes she had for herself all felt like they conspired against her.

Kim didn't win this moment because her preparation was all about her and was too one- dimensional. Winning the moment means showing up and being the best version of yourself at that point in time. One way to do this is to prepare for all possible outcomes or as many as you can. Kim was no longer catastrophizing or assuming the worst-case scenario. She was planning for how she'd like the conversation to turn out, as well as other possible outcomes. There is a difference between catastrophizing and practicing. The first time around, her one-sided strategy, which focused on how she could prove her contribution by sharing facts or data spotlighting her accomplishments, left her open to being shaken when her boss didn't respond as planned. Her preparation lacked a 360-degree perspective that responded to other outcomes. This lack of preparation disarmed Kim, shaking her ability to stay calm and feel safe when she received an unexpected response.

Kim was, in fact doing a great job and was told she had immense potential, but she was paralyzed when her boss said she wasn't ready to take the lead on an important project. Hearing this set off her instinct to catastrophize like a match hitting a bonfire. Kim's initial reflex was to run straight out of her boss's office. What was she thinking? Asking for this so soon was a terrible idea, she thought. Thankfully, she knew it was not a good idea to sprint out of her boss's office, but Kim could not think of what to say in response. Tongue-tied, she thanked her boss for listening and left.

Kim wondered why she didn't stick up for herself or respond in a more powerful way. She was understandably upset and frustrated. The reason Kim could not respond in the way she wanted was because Kim did not prepare enough for the various scenarios that could take place. She planned for an affirmative response, but what about a "maybe" or the dreaded "no"?

After I spent two years studying with former NYPD and FBI hostage negotiator Chris Voss, a man who has navigated the highest stakes and knows the cost of being unprepared, I became painfully aware of something: "When the pressure is on, you don't rise to the occasion—you fall to your highest level of preparation."

My philosophy is to prepare every day as if success is inevitable. One day, you'll be called, and you'll be ready.

The clarity of foresight, the anticipation of outcomes, the rehearsal of responses—these are the weapons in the arsenal of the prepared. World-class performers do not get caught off guard, at least not often. They are emotionally and tactically prepared for the expected and the unexpected. This requires a clear and detached vision of how to respond to desired and undesired outcomes.

You might be thinking, "Isn't planning for an undesirable outcome a form of catastrophizing?" Here's the difference. Catastrophizing is assuming an unfavorable outcome, one that you have an emotional tie to not wanting, maybe even dreading. The 360- degree, world-class preparation I'm referring to is planning and preparing without emotion or attachment to any possible responses. Assume the best but prepare for responses to the rest.

Creating a 360-Degree Preparation for Moments That Matter

Imagine you are in a movie and asked to shoot three different scenes for the same storyline. In the first scene, the director instructs you to respond when you receive the green light to your passionate plea to lead your fictional country in a peace initiative that saves the world. In the second scene, the director asks you to respond when your beloved peace initiative receives only partial buy-in and a partial budget. You did not receive a no, but you did not receive a yes, either. There is still some uncertainty. In the third and final scene, your director asks you to respond when you are firmly denied the chance to lead the peace initiative you are so passionate about. In other words, you are directed to respond to a resounding yes, a maybe, and a firm no. For each scene to turn out as powerfully as possible and for you to have the chance to lead the peace initiative for your country, you'll need to be prepared emotionally and tactically for each response. Without attachment to the outcome of the three scenes, you prepare for each scene.

There is a difference between worrying and preparation. The former imagines an outcome going wrong and fuels those thoughts with an emotional attachment to that outcome. We typically play out the scenario in our mind along with the fear, doubt, and disappointment we imagine we would feel. When we do this, we are visualizing the outcome we do not want to happen, especially when emotion is attached to our thinking (Tartakovsky 2018). From a neuropsychology perspective, the research tells us that our brain does not decipher between what's imagined and what's real. When we worry instead of preparing, there is a cascade of reactions from there that can have negative effects on our performance.

So why prepare for a less-than-desirable outcome?

Familiarity.

When we are familiar with something, we feel safe. Familiar with our jobs, our driving route home, our friends, our home, our community, and so on. The drive toward the familiar can be so strong that we choose to remain safe even though we know it's not best for us (Janssen 2024).

When we prepare rather than worry, we're like an actor in a movie with three different scenes. Therefore, the scenes are not sealed with emotion, only with possibility. Preparing for different outcomes is making sure the outcome is the best it can be, regardless of which scenario unfolds.

Planning for the Moments That Matter

For us to chart a path to where we want to go and to remain on that trajectory, we must be clear about how to show up in the moments that matter most. This will help us win the moment, especially when the stakes are high. Here's how to prepare in a way so you won't be caught off guard and allow your emotions to derail your best performance.

The ABC Prep

Often, when leading up to a high-stakes conversation or presentation, we prepare what we have to say with little regard to how the other person or persons will respond. If the response is a surprise, good or otherwise, we run the risk of our emotions being triggered (Neta & Kim, 2023) and, therefore, throwing us off our game. This is because, according to mental health expert Dr. Melanie C. Gallo, surprise can be interpreted by our brain as a threat (Gallo 2022). If a sabertoothed tiger popped out of the bushes, we would need to access our fight-or-flight response. Fortunately, when we are speaking with our boss, colleague, or customer, there may be a lot on the line, but our lives are not at risk.

Taking a 360-degree view of our response to how a situation may turn out helps us to feel familiar, stay calm, and focus on what's most important to do our best. Using ABC Prep—preparing for plans A, B, and C—will give us more agency over the result we desire and, more importantly, will allow us to show up to the best of our ability.

I used the ABC Prep method when preparing for the recent CREW (Commercial Real Estate Women) National Convention in Atlanta, where I led a mega session to a packed room of over 600 attendees. Of course, plan A was everything going as planned, and a standing ovation at the end. A Plan B outcome was a lukewarm response from the audience, and plan C was something going wrong, say me tripping on stage or losing sound or access to my slide deck. To be clear, I did mentally rehearse these things happening, I rehearsed my response to them happening without worry or emotion, which came in extremely handy for this recent national convention!

Thankfully, I did! Despite two practice runs, the audio went out just before my final exercise with the audience. Yes, there was an initial panic, but I was able to get back into the zone quickly and determine the best thing to do for myself and for the audience. I decided to do the last interactive exercise without the music to the best of my ability.

Right before I began, an amazing young woman in the audience found the song on Spotify and came to the stage with her phone! I held her phone to my lavalier with one hand, began the visualization exercise, and everyone cheered!

Here's something that no one in the audience knew. Of course, I practiced my speech for many weeks, but I also practiced my reaction for the best outcome (a standing ovation), for a mediocre outcome (a distracted audience and how to re-engage them), and for a potentially disruptive outcome (losing sound or losing access to my deck).

Plan A — for when the doors swing open with a resounding yes. Craft the perfect response that amplifies your counterpart's confidence in their affirmation. How will you proceed? What will be your first steps following this green light? How will you make him or her feel great about saying yes? For example, you buy a new high-end electric car that costs more than you want to spend. Once the salesperson gets you to sign the contract and you're done with the purchasing process, her job is not over. To create a repeat or lifelong customer and build trust, the salesperson says, "Congratulations! This vehicle will save you $6,600.00 in gas every year, keep your family safe, and it is so much better for the environment than the alternative you were considering." Maybe you've stretched a bit to buy the car, but rather than having buyer's remorse, you now feel confident and proud that you made the right decision.

Plan B — for when the response is a tentative maybe or a door left ajar, neither closed nor open. Let's say we're still at the car dealership, but this time, we are unsure if we should stretch our budget for the electric vehicle that we want. What does the salesperson say? Perhaps she acknowledges your concerns and has another question, ready to learn more about what the deeper objection is. How can she have her best shot at turning a wavering consideration into a resounding yes? How can she nudge the conversation forward? The first step is to consider her response to a split decision or partial buy-in. She might use a "caring" tone and ask a question to gain more information or allow you, the customer, to explain yourself. Something like, "It seems like the price difference between this electric vehicle and a newer version of your current vehicle is a concern?"

Plan C — for the dreaded no. When faced with rejection or a flat-out no, how will you pivot? How can you transform a no into a yes or at least limit it to a "no for now"? How will you maintain your composure and articulate your next steps? The salesperson might smile, take a deep breath, acknowledge what you, the customer, said, and offer to show you other options. It's not about courting pessimism. It's about thoroughness in your preparation. It's possible to gain more respect by demonstrating poise in the face of disappointment than by unchallenged success.

Anticipate every nuance of these defining moments. Envision your response and the potential reactions from your counterpart or counterparts that may arise. Rehearse your responses, refine your words, and practice—in a mirror if necessary—to ensure you are not just prepared but ready for almost anything.

The key to seizing the opportunity is not just to be ready but to be proactively expectant of success while also being prepared for responses to roadblocks or setbacks. This

SHERYL KLINE, M.A. CHPC

type of 360-degree preparation familiarizes you with responses to various conditions so your emotions don't override your best response.

Let's revisit our channel sales manager, Kim, after she did her 360-degree preparation with the help of the ABC Prep Worksheet™. Kim had her second one-on-one with her boss a few weeks later. Here's how Kim's ABC Prep Worksheet™ looked:

Desired Result: Total buy-in, a green light to spearhead the project.

Plan A — I receive total buy-in to lead the major initiative. My boss is confident I have the knowledge and leadership skills to keep my team accountable and productive moving forward. I'll let her know about the course I've completed to help me become more proficient in partner management, as well as the accountability process that I've created for myself and my team.

Plan B — I've made progress! My boss is open to having me lead the major initiative, but she's still on the fence as to whether I'm proficient enough in my partner management and leadership skills. I acknowledge and validate her concerns as being understandable and then let her know, like with Plan A, my completed coursework and accountability structure, as well as a leadership training that I've completed. I've also prepared a smaller ask: to be able to create and present a proposed action plan and timeline.

Plan C — I'm prepared to respond to a no, and I'm confident that I can still make progress in this conversation. What is important to my boss, and what can shift my boss's response to a yes?

What are one or two hard data points or facts that are meaningful to my boss that I can share to boost her confidence in me and what I'm asking? What are possible reasons that would make her say no, and what will I need to do to debunk those reasons or make my boss feel safe and confident enough to say yes? If my boss is a firm no, what will be the best way to exit the conversation so I can come back and try again at another time and have a good shot at making progress?

What about you?

Desired result: What is your next most important conversation, presentation, or interaction? How do you want it to turn out?:

_____

_____

_____

Plan A — What is the most positive response/outcome, and how will you make the other person/people feel good about their decision?

_____

_____

_____

Plan B — What could a tentative or partial buy- in look like, and how might you respond? (The Influence chapter will help with tentative decisions. Do your best here, and you can refine your response later.)

_____

_____

_____

Plan C — If your idea or contribution is rejected, what might the reason or objection be, and how can you prepare ahead of time with hard data or facts for this response?

_____

_____

_____

Remember, you are practicing your response (not your reaction) to these different scenarios, not imagining the full scenario playing out in your mind. If you choose to attach emotion to your practice, be sure it is calm, confident, or even grateful. Your tone will mimic your thoughts (Lickerman, 2010). As you practice Plan A, B, and C, be sure to feel the outcome you'd like before you attempt to speak your response. Our feelings about certain situations are more important than you might think.

While our conscious minds can handle about 40 to 50 bits of information per second, the human body sends approximately 11 million bits of information to our brains every second (Markowsky, 2024). In other words, if we feel fearful, anxious, or in danger (of not getting the job, not getting the raise, getting reprimanded by our boss) or if we are surprised by an outcome or response, we are flooded with signals that trigger danger. If we feel a certain way, it's likely that we will express this feeling by our tone, cadence of our speech, or body language, either consciously or unconsciously.

"Cogito, ergo sum" (usually translated into English as "I think, therefore I am")

—*René Descartes*

Preparing for your responses to alternate outcomes or different scenarios will help you stay focused and think like a world-class performer. You'll be able to say what you mean and mean what you say while remaining congruent to the best version of yourself.

For example, imagine you are preparing for your one-to-one monthly meeting with your boss, and you'll be sharing an idea to streamline marketing efforts and drive more revenue. Your idea is a bit unconventional and outside the status quo, but you have done your research and believe in your idea wholeheartedly. Your boss, however, has been with the company for 15 years and can be resistant to painting outside the lines.

Plan A — What is the most positive response/outcome, and how will you make the other person/people feel good about their decision?

_____

_____

_____

Your boss's response is, "That's a great idea. Nice job. You have the green light to move forward. Please show me your proposal by Thursday next week."

In order to make your boss feel confident and therefore safe about his decision, respond with outcomes that are important to him, such as, "Fantastic. Here's the outline, accountability structure, and research behind why this strategy is solid and should help drive the growth you're looking for this half.

If you were not prepared, your initial reaction may be one of shock or dismay because you are so used to receiving resistance. You might stumble over your words because you were caught off guard, even if in a good way. Let's make sure that does not happen. World-class preparation for a yes is just as important as for a no.

Plan B — What could a tentative decision or partial buy-in look like, and how might you respond? This time, your boss responds with, "Your idea makes sense to me, and I'm inclined to consider it. Unfortunately, the timing isn't ideal."

_____

_____

_____

You'll learn more about how to respond to a tentative decision in the Influence chapter, but for now, do your best here and be sure to think through and practice your best response. A hint is to start with acknowledging and validating your boss's position and making sure you have facts to back up your ask. This would be a great time to gather more information as well (which could be very helpful later). You might say, "Seems like we're on the same page when it comes to a new growth plan. What about the timing is not ideal?"

_____

_____

_____

Plan C — Your boss rejects your request, says it makes no sense, and there is no budget anyway. If your idea or contribution is rejected or you get a flat no, what might the reason be, and how can you prepare ahead of time with hard data or facts for such a response?

_____

_____

With little to no preparation for this response, it is extremely easy to get emotional, angry (he never listens to me), frightened (maybe it was a bad idea), or frustrated (I don't feel heard). This is extremely understandable. By practicing your various responses, you have walked the course before. In other words, you are familiar with each response without emotional attachment or surprise and prepared to respond in the best way possible. Emotions are not spiked, at least not as much, and you have your best shot at staying zoned in for your best performance.

SECTION 2

Confidence:
Own Your Shift

Do you remember when you were a Senior in high school? If it was a millennium ago like it was for me, perhaps it's easier to think about someone you know who is or was recently in high school. Either way, seniors in high school are leaders of the pack. They've been around the block for the past few years, know the campus, know the teachers, know what's expected, and are much more experienced than freshmen. At least until they are sent back to freshman status again in college, in an apprenticeship, in a job, or in whatever their next placement as an adult is. Back they go to the discomfort of the unfamiliar. This process of familiarity, followed by the unfamiliar, can ebb and flow throughout our lives.

My 24-year-old daughter explained her feelings after college as though the guidebook she'd been given for her life up to this point ended abruptly, and there was no such guidebook for her next steps. She was confident and familiar in college, had friends, and knew what was expected. With a new job and friends going in different directions, she was a freshman again, this time at "adulting."

Change can be exhilarating and terrifying all at the same time. Sometimes, we realize the gift of change immediately, and sometimes, it's not until time has passed that we've had time to reflect.

Confidence is not static. Many of us have likely experienced our confidence getting rattled by a new job, project, employment status, or promotion. Confidence is also commonly misconceived as an innate trait, but in truth, it is a skill shaped by upbringing, experience, and action. It is not reserved for the fortunate few; it is an acquirable and essential skill, even in the face of new challenges or intense pressure.

Confidence may ebb and flow, particularly in unfamiliar territory or during pivotal moments like going after a promotion or experiencing a significant change. Yet its fluidity is a strength—it means that as circumstances evolve, so too can your confidence.

If you're looking to become a champion at something new, what will make you world-class is your willingness to be vulnerable and uncomfortable and to be a freshman again.

When she was not much older than a college freshman, Gavriella Schuster, the prominent technology leader and now board chairman at Microsoft, decided she'd embody champion qualities at a very young age. Gavriella did not begin her career, dreaming of becoming a corporate vice president at Microsoft. That was well beyond what she imagined success to be. For Gavriella, success meant finding joy in what she was doing, making an impact, empowering others to bring their best, remaining authentic to herself, her integrity, and her values, and making enough money to feel comfortable. Success did not include a job title, or scope of responsibility — after she made it to general manager at Microsoft, she felt fulfilled and believed she had achieved everything she wanted. When she got promoted, though, it opened a whole new world for her to have an even greater impact.

What inspired Gavriella in the mid-1990s to work hard as the only woman in the room much of the time? It was the fear of becoming like her father. Gavriella witnessed her father simply rise through the ranks at the same organization for more than 25 years.

He was very comfortable in his role and was afraid of change. At the age of 50, her father was laid off, and with his job went his identity. A junior in college at that time, Gavriella realized her father's entire identity and ego were wrapped up in his job. And he had been doing the same thing for so long, so he lacked the resilience to adjust and pivot to something new. Gavriella did not want to be like that and so from the time she started working professionally, her goal was to keep learning new things. This conviction gave her the strength and willingness to embrace feeling vulnerable, uncomfortable, or "like a freshman" again. To build resilience and as much equity for

SHERYL KLINE, M.A. CHPC

herself as she was building for the organization where she worked.

There were many times along the way that Gavriella questioned her own approach, particularly when she would find herself in a job where she felt unqualified. But each experience brought resilience and clarity that she was, in fact, in the right place at the right time.

Here are a few key lessons Gavriella learned to gain Confidence each step of the way:

- Define what is important to you, set boundaries, and don't cross them.
- Know your own values, find your voice, and stand up for what you believe in.
- Define what success means to you, and don't get caught up in everyone else's definition of success.

Reflection:

What person or experience can you draw upon to help you gain confidence? Is there someone you admire or someone who has had a challenge that fuels your drive for what's next?

_____

_____

_____

Confidence is not just a feeling; it is an identity. Confidence is the undercurrent of our interactions, the silent song that plays in the background of our dreams and actions, and, therefore, the unseen force that can shape our reality. With confidence, our voice carries not just words but intentions, aspirations, and our inner truth. Without it, our voice can be like a boulder that blocks the path for us to move forward, no matter how hard we push.

What we think inevitably influences the actions we take and ultimately, our reality (Adapt for Life 2024). The voice we tend to listen to is our own because it's constant and we've been listening to it the longest. To be perceived by others as confident, we must be confident. Internal confidence is the precursor to the conviction others will have in us, our abilities, and our ideas.

If we are not confident in ourselves, our unspoken and sometimes even unconscious cues can signal a lack of confidence. How can someone else be confident in us, our ideas, or our opinions if we are not confident in ourselves? How you say something is often more impactful than what you say, and the driver of how you say it will depend on how confident you feel.

Confidence is fluid like the tide coming in and going out. Learning how to be emotionally agile and how to be the observer and not the judge will help when riding the waves, so you aren't smacked down by a six-foot wave like I was the last time I went surfing. Confidence can also be predictable or unpredictable, particularly when we are in uncharted territory at pivotal moments. Being able to manage this fluidity and learn to use the current as power is a strength—it means that as circumstances evolve, so too can your confidence.

To elevate our confidence and the confidence others have in us, let's jump into the following four world-class tools proven to help you show up and deliver your best, even when under pressure or during periods of change.

SHERYL KLINE, M.A. CHPC

CHAPTER 6

Own Your Voice

Do you remember when you were a young child, and your mother or father would say, "You should speak to your parents, teachers, grandparents, and other adults with kindness and respect." I distinctly remember in my teenage years being told by my mother not to speak to her in a "sassy tone." I'm sure I gave her the same eye-rolling that my daughter gave me when I voiced the same thing a couple of years back.

Do you remember being told the tone to use when speaking to yourself? I certainly do not remember hearing that I should speak to myself with a respectful or kind tone. And that's unfortunate because our internal dialog and how it's delivered is extremely powerful. It can be a built-in cheering section that inspires us to keep going, to throw our hat into the ring for a stretch role, or ask for a raise that we know we deserve. Or it can be a bully that calls us an imposter, unworthy, or that tears us down, causing us not to speak up.

The voice that we've been listening to the longest is our

own, so our brain pays close attention. This power we wield can directly impact our behavior, perception of ourselves, and the actions we take (Adapt for Life, 2024). We can be our worst critics, inflicting shame, doubt, and even disgust that sting far greater than the sticks and stones others fling. Flipping your internal voice's script is an important way to become more confident in your next level of impact as a leader.

Your internal voice, what you think over and over, and the emotions you tie to these thoughts inevitably influence what you project to others. For others to be confident in you, you must first be confident in yourself.

Albert Mehrabian, a University of California at Los Angeles researcher and professor, coined the 7-38- 55 rule of communication. Only seven percent of what we communicate is derived from spoken words, while 38 percent comes from tone and a significant 55 percent from body language. This highlights that how you say something is often more impactful than what you say. For example, if we are doubtful of our ability or if we are unsure of the validity of our contribution, it could be challenging for others to be confident in us.

So, how do you transform your internal monologue from a critic to a coach? Let's look at one story of an incredible computer scientist who used her internal voice to fuel her external success, helping her build the confidence to become a visionary pioneer in her field. Since Dr. Ayanna Howard was truly a pioneer, her internal monologue could have been full of fear, doubt, and frustration. "No one else has done this, so how can I possibly do it?" or "Will it be too difficult?" Ayanna's internal monologue did not consist of those questions, or if it ever did, it was not for long.

Ayanna was born in Providence, Rhode Island, and eventually relocated with her mother and father to Pasadena, California. She was fascinated with the 1980s television series The Bionic Woman, which was about a woman who was severely injured and put back together using bionic limbs that gave her superpowers. At a young age, Ayanna wanted to be a doctor, but biology— or, more specifically, dissecting frogs—did not suit her. However, once she discovered robotics and engineering, she was hooked.

Ayanna did not have many women, let alone Black women, to serve as professional role models for her. She instead became her own role model along the way with the mantra, "Your best champion and cheerleader is yourself. Always be proud of your accomplishments, big or small." This mantra shaped her internal voice and kept her focused on what was important to her, shielding her from the naysayers and self-doubt.

Today, Ayanna is a powerhouse and world- renowned expert in technology and engineering. She is a tenured professor and was the first woman to become a dean at Ohio State University. She has worked for the NASA Jet Propulsion Laboratory, where she was instrumental in creating the autonomous robots that collect data on Mars. Among her many other achievements, she founded Zyrobotics, a company that creates mobile therapy and educational products for children with special needs. Her accomplishments are not just personal triumphs but milestones in changing the narrative for women and minorities in STEM fields.

Women like Ayanna, who are pioneers, often face barriers that their male counterparts, or less marginalized female counterparts, rarely encounter. Without having role models or colleagues who looked like her, her internal monologue could have led her down a path of frustration and doubt. But it didn't. We, too, can pay more attention to our intuition. We can listen to our internal voice that tells us we are powerful and to keep going, that we are good enough worthy, and that our leadership is needed now. Our internal voice can be trained to tell us to keep striving instead of accepting the status quo. This will deflect the naysayers and shatter previous beliefs of what we thought was possible for ourselves. That is if you know how to harness its power to support you and not succumb to its power to destroy you.

Your internal voice is sometimes a whisper and sometimes a roar—a declaration of intent, a banner under which we rally our personal strengths to face the seemingly impossible. If you are aware of your internal voice or of the monologue that runs in your mind when it's your time to speak up, make a shift, or try something new, it can be your greatest guide to your deepest desires.

To hear this voice, try slowing time by taking silent walks in nature, meditating, or just being still. You may hear career insights, such as "I'd love to try working in the supply chain, but my education and experience is in consulting" (true story). It's in these still moments that clues appear. Our job is to capture and document them before our head tells us that we're crazy or that what we are thinking doesn't make sense. Most who have reached an extremely difficult destination have confronted moments when their goals seemed ludicrous, yet they chose to proceed anyway. We have more power than we may realize to use our internal voice to champion or destroy our dreams.

World-class performers, despite their veneer of

invincibility, grapple with doubt and uncertainty just like anyone else, as do members of your leadership team and board from time to time. The difference between world-class performers and everyone else is their refusal to remain stuck in negative thinking or paralyzed by self-doubt. World-class leaders, whether in athletics, in business, or in any other endeavor, know how to harness these negative thoughts and transform them into catalysts for growth and action.

To shift your internal monologue from one of doubt to one of determination involves crafting a declaration—a bold affirmation of your objectives and the confidence with which you intend to achieve them.

Your Internal Declaration

Consider the power of a declaration, an inner voice that is commanding your success, one that includes the minute details—the setting, the feeling, the emotions, and every way it will impact you and others. These details are not frivolous; they are the very fabric of your future reality. They anchor your goals in the tangible world and make them more attainable. The tone of a declaration is that of a commander who is decisive, who administers a plan with confidence, and who makes us feel like everything will work out and that victory is inevitable if we stay committed to the process.

Let's take my declaration as an example. Four years before it happened, I declared to myself that I would speak at the United Nations Leadership Conference. This was a thought that came to me when I was out for a run with my black Labrador, Kona. When I got home, before I allowed my mind to talk me out of this seemingly crazy idea, I wrote down that I would speak at the UN within four years. I also drew (I use this term lightly as I am no artist) myself on a stage, my kids sitting behind me, and the same well-lit, vast gathering space typically used for diplomats and dignitaries. This wasn't just an ambition; it was an inner monologue painted with precision and emotion. It included the act of speaking but also the presence of my children, the connection with the audience, and the focus of each listener in the audience. This visualization wasn't idle daydreaming; it was a strategic rehearsal for a future I later realized when I was invited to speak at a leadership conference at the United Nations in 2023. A declaration is a tool that shapes your internal landscape and what is possible for you, directing your focus away from the negative and toward courage, control, and confidence. It's an exercise in cognitive redirection, creating a reality that does not exist in the present time but one you believe has already happened in the future. The reframing of your inner monologue bolsters your belief in what is possible.

However, maintaining an optimistic internal voice doesn't mean ignoring fear, doubt, setbacks, or worry when they arise. It means consciously choosing which narratives to amplify and which ones to turn down the volume on. External factors, such as family members, colleagues, and friends, can have a significant impact on your internal monologue. Sometimes, the people who care about us the most will intentionally or unintentionally box us in, thinking it will keep us safe or for any other host of reasons. "Don't leave your current job and a steady paycheck in search of a role you really love," they might say. Alternatively, you may have champions in your life who say, "You are capable of making a pivot. You've done it before. How can I help?" You have control over both dials—which external voices to turn up and which to turn down.

Since external voices, especially from those who are closest to you, can have such a powerful impact on your internal monologue, it may be time to consider who you are spending the most time with. For example, my son switched tennis clubs two years ago. He is a former college tennis player who, at the time, was just beginning his career as a certified financial analyst. He wanted to find other tennis players of a similar level as him and network, build friendships, and find mentors. I was sad to see him leave our club, but the club he found has proven to be a better haven for all of the things he wanted. As it turned out, the members of his new tennis club were not only great players, but they also improved my son's internal voice by providing career advice and sharing their experiences.

Reflection:

Which of my friends, family members, colleagues, or acquaintances should I spend more time with because they will impact my internal voice and my belief system in a positive way? Whose volume should I turn down or distance myself from?

_____

_____

_____

If you cannot think of anyone, think about a group to join, a class to take, or organizations to get involved with where you are likely to find the types of people you'd like to spend more time with.

The most persuasive voice you will ever hear is your

own—it drives your motivation, molds your behavior, and ultimately shapes your destiny. It can be influenced by who you spend the most time with, so make sure you choose wisely and spend time with those who will lift you up, push you forward, and offer support when possible.

The Power of Your Internal Voice

Your internal voice is the driver behind the actions you take and the ones you don't, the challenges you accept and the ones you decline, the opportunities you seize, and the ones you shy away from. It is the voice that will urge you to speak up in meetings or to stay quiet, that will advocate for your ideas, and that will push you to apply for roles or dissuade you from doing so. It is the voice that says, "I am worthy. I am capable. I am ready. I can and I will."

Will fear, doubt, and worry creep in from time to time? Absolutely. But to own our shift, let's learn how to create Olympic-level inner monologues that lift us up and never destroy our dreams or even slow them down.

Ready to do the work so you can have a world- class inner voice? Let's craft an internal monologue that is kind, assertive, and encouraging. Let's ensure that when you speak to yourself, you do so with the wisdom, compassion, and conviction that will make your internal voice an unshakeable foundation for your success.

Own Your Shift Model™

The Own Your Shift Model™ is a worksheet that will help you shift what you say and how you say it so you can close the gap between who you are today and who you'd like to become or what you'd like to achieve.

It is a tool to help you shift your internal monologue, so you feel like you've already accomplished what you desire. This, in turn, helps you to embody the future leader you'd like to become and take on her persona and her confidence today.

It is also important to note that your "shift" may not be something big or monumental. Perhaps you are a manager who has been doing a really good job, but you'd like your next project to be more world class along with how you present the results. That is still an important shift.

Keep in mind that confidence is a learned skill that can enable you to show up and deliver and give you the conviction to keep going, especially when the road gets difficult. It's vital we have an optimistic inner voice so that we can believe what we want and deserve is possible. To own our shift, we must decide which story our mind chooses to hear. Remember: the voice we tend to listen to the most is our own, and it's a significant driver of our motivation and confidence.

Let's ensure your internal voice fuels your next level of success and joy.

Download the Own Your Shift Model here: **http://bit.ly/ownyourshiftmodel**.

List three vivid details about your long-term objectives. For example, "I'm leading a new initiative that gives me great visibility and has a tremendous impact on the business," "My leadership listens and champions my ideas," or "I feel confident and optimistic about my contribution and future opportunities."

_____

_____

_____

Try summarizing your vivid details like these:

1. visibility/impact.
2. leadership listens/champions to my ideas.
3. feel confident about future opportunities.

What about you? What are three vivid details for your long-term objective?

_____

_____

_____

Since the voice we have been listening to the longest is our own. Like anything else, it is a process to learn and adjust, especially when we are creating a new vision for ourselves.

Reflection:

What tone would you take toward a friend if she was recently let go from her company and now found herself back on the job market or if that same friend made a mistake on an important project? How would it differ from how you'd speak to yourself in the same situation?

C H A P T E R 7

Emotional Agility

"A crazy thing happened—the very act of doing the thing
that scared me undid the fear. It's amazing the power of one
word. 'Yes' changed my life. 'Yes' changed me."
— *Shonda Rhimes, TV Producer and Screenwriter, TED2016*
(February 2016), author of 'Year of Yes

**Whether you are a tennis fan or not, you may
remember in 2020 when 17-time Grand Slam champion
Novak Djokovic was ejected from the U.S. Open.** Novak was
unable to hold serve as his opponent, Pablo Carreño Busta,
broke through for a 6 to 5 lead and would potentially be
serving for the set. In frustration, Novak attempted to hit a
stray ball into the empty stands, but he inadvertently hit a line
judge on the throat. Even though he immediately apologized
to her, Novak was ejected from the tournament.

I share this story to illustrate how fear prevents us from
succeeding. You might be wondering what Novak Djokovic's
anger has to do with fear. As it turns out, a lot.

Anger emerges when we feel threatened—emotionally, physically, financially, or in other ways. At the root of many angry feelings is a sense of powerlessness. That's why athletes who are number 1 in the world seem angry when they start losing. There is a lot on the line and nowhere for them to go, but down if they lose. Their number 1 status is being threatened, along with a host of other things, such as endorsements. Even though we may not be competing in an elite sporting event like the Grand Slam, we can still experience similar fear-based anger. When we are unable to correct or improve a situation—a traffic jam, a job loss, a relationship breakup, a chronic illness—our frustration, sadness, letdown, and other negative emotions often converge into anger. (Harvard Health Publishing, 2024).

We may not be so inclined to throw something across the room and accidentally injure our boss or colleague like Novak did, but fear-based anger or any other negative emotion, such as doubt or frustration, can certainly cloud our better judgment. It can cause us to clam up when we'd like to speak or become upset or annoyed, which will not likely help our cause. To make matters worse, angry women are not viewed favorably and tend to lose influence, while men are less affected and can even gain influence when they appear angry.

(Derra, 2015).

In this section on Emotional Agility, we'll learn to recognize our emotions and regulate them so we can use them to our advantage. We will begin to observe fear as a different character. Fear will transition from a hooded stranger in a dark alley following too closely behind us to a long-time friend we trust and who alerts us of an opportunity or prompts us to speak up. The sabertoothed tiger that threatens our lives will become a trusted guide who has the wisdom to help us. We will become the grateful observer and not the skittish judge.

The Constant Chatter and Its Impact on Our Emotions

On average, we speak over 16,000 words out loud each day, so imagine how many thoughts we have! That is an immense amount of internal monologue. According to research, the average person can have as many as 60,000 thoughts per day. Of those thousands of thoughts, 80 percent are negative, and 95 percent are exactly the same repetitive thoughts as the day before. (Swaminathan 2007).

If we add in an event that spikes our emotions in a negative way or an event that is perceived as negative, we run the risk of our emotions becoming a run-away train of negative thoughts. Let's say we get up the nerve to speak up to our boss about a bold idea, ask for a raise, or speak up in a meeting only to be denied or shut down. We may assume our idea is off, or our boss thought it was a bad idea and feels our status on our team is threatened. Maybe the very thing that triggers negative emotions is not even external. For example, Sue (not her real name) was preparing for her third round of interviews. It was a panel interview with three leaders present. That, combined with her past dozen interviews where she was a "close second," had Sue swirling in self-doubt, what-ifs, and thoughts of being rejected even before she entered the room.

This lack of emotional agility or ability to do her best when under pressure and recover quickly from negative thoughts is like being in a jungle full of potential threats but also opportunities for beauty. If we are afraid and tell ourselves stories about what lurks around the corner, we cannot access what we know to help lead us down the path to a crystal-clear lake that we'd love to see. To get there, we need to remain calm and optimistic so we can remember which way to turn, how to follow the trail markers, and how to focus on what is truly most important to ward off potential predators.

Imagine if our mind was worried and distracted by all the horrible what-ifs that could happen. Do you think it would be more likely we'd miss a turn or miss a cue to avoid walking down a certain path?

Let's learn about one iconic leader who was able to use fear to guide herself through the twists and turns in her life and career from a young age.

Fear As a Gift

Remember Gavriella Schuster? She's the former Microsoft corporate vice president who influenced the growth of over $1 trillion in ecosystem revenue, leading to 90,000 Microsoft partners and over 12,000 published marketplace solutions. She delivered over $40 billion annually in direct global partner sales revenues as well as launched and grew the Cloud Solution Provider program, licensing revenues to reach $10 billion annually over a four-year period. This is only a partial list of Gavriella's accomplishments at Microsoft. She is also a TEDx speaker, board director, and PE advisor for Open Systems, Mimecast, Nerdio, Included, Berkshire Partners, and West River Group. Gavriella is also an ATHENA Leadership Award winner, has published a training on ALLIES, and is co-founder of Women in Cloud and the Women in Technology Network.

Our ability to be emotionally agile to embrace fear, especially under pressure or when the stakes are high, is what will guide our choices, decisions, and ultimately, our destiny. The A.D.D. Emotional Agility Blueprint™ shows how to get and stay in the zone where our best decisions and performances are realized.

The A.D.D. acronym stands for:

1. **A**wareness: Notice any feelings or thoughts that are present.
2. **D**istance: Shift your thoughts from "I am ..." to "I notice ..."
3. **D**ecide the one or two most important things under my control that I will practice and focus on.

Here's a more detailed description of the A.D.D. Emotional Agility Blueprint™ so you can begin to learn how to harness your emotions for your benefit:

A.D.D. Emotional Agility Blueprint: Awareness and the Power of Presence

Since we are only capable of consciously processing a small fraction of the input we take in, most bits of information go unnoticed. This is a good thing! If we reacted to the 11 million bits of information per second that we take in, we

142

would not be able to function at all. This number is whittled down to about 40 bits of discernible information, which is much more manageable for our cognitive thinking. A simple example is when we are thinking of buying a new white Jeep SUV, and we suddenly see them all over the road and highway. Of course, we are also seeing other vehicle models and colors, but we've told our brain that the white Jeep SUV is important, so we filter out the rest.

Take, for instance, Alexia (not her real name). A seasoned vice president of sales, Alexia is accustomed to high-stakes environments. Yet, she is not immune to the flutter of nerves before a major deal is closed. With an acute awareness of why she felt the way she did and a strategy to get back into her zone, Alexia spotted the telltale signs of her fear. Rather than capitulating to the unease or throwing fuel on it, she witnessed the emotion with a nod of acknowledgment—a

silent affirmation that while anxiety is present, it was not a threat. She said, "I acknowledge you, fear, and you are not a threat." There is a small yet mighty distinction here. Alexia acknowledged the fear without saying, "I am afraid." In our mind, this distinction is the difference between being the observer of an emotion ("I acknowledge") and accepting it as truth ("I am").

When we acknowledge, we create distance and time to choose how to get back in the zone and how to proceed toward our highest integrity. When we say, "I am," we are self-labeling and accepting the emotion as truth. We cannot discern the value of emotion nor show up as our best when negative emotions have us trapped in uncertainty.

Once fear or other negative emotions are acknowledged, a light is shined in their dark little corner, and they begin to lose their power once they are exposed. Like a crystal hides unnoticed in an unassuming rock, the wisdom of fear can emerge once its emotion is neutralized.

Sometimes, our emotions are triggered by someone being unreasonable (your boss raising his/her voice) or an event that is perceived as a threat (losing your job or being denied a raise or promotion). How do we neutralize these emotions so we can figure out our best path forward?

A.D.D. Emotional Agility Blueprint: Distance

"Be the observer, not the judge."

The answer lies in the distance between you and your emotions. If we say things like; I am so angry, I am so frustrated, I am so worried, etc., we have self-labeled and accepted these emotions as truth. We are like the most absorbent sponge that soaks up all the water that spills on the counter when the cup is tipped over. Left unattended, this absorbent sponge eventually hits its capacity to absorb any more water and stops working. If you have ever experienced a time when several emotional events occur, you know how easy it is to snap. Say a friendship needs repairing, and then your boss reprimands you, and then when you get home, your partner lashes out at you. Snap! The straw that breaks the camel's back is due to a lack of awareness and ability to regulate emotions. What ensues is a reaction that is likely a departure from the highest version of ourselves. Eventually, when we do regulate our emotions, we likely owe someone an apology, which never seems to feel good nor get us what we want.

By becoming aware and learning to regulate our emotions we can make a conscious and strategic choice in the moment of how to act rather than reacting in a way that's incongruent with our best selves. Whenever you have an important conversation, presentation, or any high-stakes interaction, part of your preparation can be to check in with yourself to observe how you are feeling. Having A.D.D. Emotional Agility checkpoints in the middle of and just prior to ending important interactions can be extremely helpful in making course corrections so you can stay in the zone.

For example, you may have a sticky note on your computer that says Breathe or Focus on the Facts. At half past the hour, it may be helpful to look at your sticky note as a reminder to take back control of your mindset and get back in the zone. This way you'll be more likely to respond with your highest integrity and not react out of unharnessed emotion.

Raising our awareness and noticing how we're feeling rather than embodying the feeling creates space between ourselves and that emotion. It serves as a safeguard, allowing us to act with deliberation rather than react to emotional triggers. Creating distance versus self-labeling ourselves with our emotions is like standing on the bank of a running river rather than choosing to step in and be tossed around. Observe the turbulent water, have gratitude and respect for its strength, but remain on the bank so you can choose how to proceed in the best way possible rather than get tossed around uncontrollably.

It's not that top performers are immune to difficulties, setbacks, and negative emotions like fear, doubt, frustration, and even anger at times. The key is knowing how to use those powerful emotions as fuel to amplify your success rather than disable it. Taking control of your mindset and deciding your next best move is a helpful way to do just that.

A.D.D. Emotional Agility Blueprint: Decide: Control What You Can That's Most Important

Phonetically, de-cide means "death of." The only one who gets to decide what you can accomplish, if you're worthy, if you're capable, or if you will ever achieve a dream is YOU. You also get to decide how you will perform in a meeting, presentation, or any high-stakes interaction.

But you must decide how you'd like an interaction to turn out and then do the work to make it happen. You decide that your long-term objective has already happened, you decide to improve, and you commit to your short-term objectives by doing them consistently for a certain period of time.

The essence of being able to decide is the assertive act of making choices that resonate with our innermost aspirations and core values. It's about steering our ship with conviction, guided by our North Star, not the unpredictable winds of circumstance.

Deciding becomes a strategic navigation tool on a journey marked by resilience and adaptability. It's a conscious alignment of our intentions with our actions, preparing to tackle the hurdles along the path and maintain course fidelity amid the unpredictability of life's twists, turns, and uncertainty.

Reflection:

Is there something in your past that you were fearful of but, in hindsight, was a gift? If so, what was it, and how was it helpful? If not, is there anything coming up that makes you feel fearful? How could you look at it from a different perspective, and what is a lesson you could learn from it?

_____

_____

_____

Now It's YOUR Turn:

1. "A" awareness of the "red" emotions (anger, fear, doubt, frustration) that may arise in regard to an upcoming crucial conversation, presentation, or interaction.

List an example of an upcoming high-pressure/important situation that matters to you and the emotion you may feel in association with it. (for example, "Meeting with my boss again regarding a raise." "Feeling frustrated."

_____

_____

_____

2. "D" distance yourself from the emotion that no longer serves you. Take three deep belly breaths in through your nose and out through your mouth. On the inhale, see the emotion coming towards you, and on the exhale, see the emotion passing through you. Write a sentence that creates distance between you and your emotions. (e.g., "I notice a feeling of frustration when I'm not being heard" instead of "I am frustrated when I'm not being heard.")

_____

_____

_____

3. "D" decide what action is most important that you have control over. What is it, and when will you take action? For example, "I'll schedule a one-on-one with my colleague who is constantly interrupting me."

From Feeling Stuck to Deciding What's Next

Emily, an aspiring leader, found herself standing at the crossroads of an important decision. She wondered if it was best to focus on the qualities that she thought were required for a role or focus on what she knew made her a strong candidate. With an unwavering knowledge of the qualities and authenticity she brings to the table, Emily chose to emphasize these strengths in the application for her new role, placing faith and feeling in her authenticity.

What almost held Emily back from sharing this authenticity was fear. While she was confident that she could get up to speed quickly, she was afraid that she could not check all the boxes for the role and, therefore, put herself in jeopardy of losing it. She was also afraid of appearing like she was bragging about her strengths. Rather than self-labeling, she distanced herself from these thoughts. Rather than thinking, "I am underqualified, and I am someone who brags too much," she shifted to, "I notice that I feel like I'm not qualified and that I feel like I'm bragging when I emphasize what I love doing as well as what I'm good at." Shifting from "I am" to "I notice" may seem like a small shift, but the impact it has on our perspective is enormous. When we say, "I am," we are self-labeling. It's definitive. Remember, the voice we pay attention to the most is our own. If we say we are not qualified, we aren't. When we say, "I notice," we become the observer. This distance creates the space we need to ask the important questions: "Do I know this to be true?" or "Would it be a good idea to get another perspective from someone who cares about me and who knows my work ethic and capabilities?" "Let's say I do apply. What would be my first best step?"

When Emily became the observer of what she was feeling and noticed her thoughts and feelings rather than labeling herself, she was able to make an objective decision about whether she would apply. The statements she was previously telling herself were not, in fact true, and her previous experience was validated by her past mentor. Emily decided to apply. She determined her first step was to find out who the hiring manager was and what she was looking for in a candidate. Emily was able to step out of the rushing river and stop getting tossed around by her mind so she could stand on the bank and make a decision.

Deciding becomes a navigation strategy on a journey

marked by resilience and adaptability. It's a conscious alignment of our intentions with our actions so we can tackle the hurdles along the path and maintain course fidelity amid the unpredictability of life's twists, turns, and uncertainties.

Not Just for Work, for Life

The Emotional Agility A.D.D Blueprint is more than a high-performance framework for our careers. It teaches us to engage with our emotions not as adversaries but as guides and catalysts for growth. Through this blueprint, we become the architects of what actions we take and how we show up, crafting our destinies with intention and purpose.

Emotional Agility, therefore, emerges as the linchpin of successful leadership. It doesn't shun emotions but navigates them with poise and strategy. It is about immersing oneself in the tapestry of human experience and using every thread, every color, to weave a narrative of fearless leadership that resonates with authenticity and influences with grace. This journey toward Emotional Agility is one of embracing the full spectrum of our emotions as valuable tools.

In the pursuit of Emotional Agility, it is essential to remember that this journey is both personal and communal. It is about the individual leader's growth and about nurturing an environment where every member of the team can thrive emotionally and professionally.

Embracing Emotional Agility means recognizing the power of vulnerability as a leader. By sharing our own experiences with fear, doubt, or excitement, we humanize the leadership experience, making it accessible and relatable. This openness becomes a guidepost for others, encouraging them to share their journeys, which can foster a culture of mutual support and collective resilience.

The practice of Emotional Agility also involves celebrating the small victories along the way. In a high-pressure, results-driven environment, it's easy to overlook the incremental progress we make each day.

Acknowledging and affirming small victories not only bolsters our confidence but also encourages a mindset of continual growth and learning within our teams.

As leaders, our Emotional Agility becomes a model for others, showcasing how to turn challenges into opportunities for growth and innovation. By mastering this skill, we demonstrate how to leverage emotional insights for strategic decision-making, how to communicate with impact and empathy, and how to inspire and mobilize teams toward a shared vision.

Emotional Agility is more than just a tool; it is a transformative approach that redefines the essence of leadership. It invites us to step into our power, to lead not just with our minds but with our hearts, and to forge a path of leadership that is as courageous as it is compassionate. It is about making a conscious choice, day after day, to lead not only with the strength of our convictions but also with the depth of our humanity.

Case Study: Architecture — Zoe's Urban Development Project

Zoe, the lead architect at an innovative architecture firm, faced the high-stakes challenge of presenting a sustainable urban development project to skeptical stakeholders.

Emotional Agility Application: Prior to her presentation, Zoe anticipated feeling nervous and used the A.D.D Emotional Agility Blueprint to pre-emptively address these emotions. She focused on awareness by acknowledging her anxiety, distanced herself from negativity by redirecting her thoughts toward the potentially positive impact of the project, and decided to concentrate on her strengths, such as her expertise in sustainable design.

Outcome: Zoe's presentation was not only met with interest but also sparked a valuable discussion on sustainable urban planning, leading to the green lighting of her project.

Case Study: Legal Tech Innovations— Jacqueline's Software Launch

Jacqueline, a legal tech entrepreneur, was about to launch an AI-based software to streamline legal processes.

Emotional Agility Application: Understanding the pressure and doubt that comes with launching a tech product, Jacqueline embraced the ADD Emotional Agility Blueprint to navigate her wide range of emotions effectively. She remained acutely aware of her stress levels, created a mental distance from negative self-talk, and decided to focus on actionable steps like final software tests and marketing strategies.

Outcome: Despite the many ups and downs of the project, the software launch exceeded expectations, with Jacqueline's emotional agility playing a key role in her ability to lead her team confidently through the launch phase.

Becoming emotionally agile is not a set-and- forget strategy. It's more about self-regulation, especially when the stakes are high or when there's a lot on the line. The Emotional Wheel ™ is a visual gauge and guidepost to help you become aware of your emotions and manage the ups and downs so you can focus on your best performance.

SHERYL KLINE, M.A. CHPC

C H A P T E R 8

Emotional Agility Part 2:
The Emotional Wheel

For better or worse, our meetings, presentations, performance reviews, and customer interactions are rarely, if ever, predictable. Like an Olympian, our aim is to show up in a world-class way during important interactions. We don't want to choke under pressure, allowing emotions to drive behavior that we later regret.

Whether alone or as part of a team, by becoming emotionally agile we can get and stay in the zone for optimal performance. This is where creativity, productivity, innovation, and team cohesion arise (Andersyn, 2023). When we or our colleagues are emotionally dysregulated, individual and team performance suffers, and there is a risk of emotional tax as well as plummeting productivity, innovation, and, ultimately, profitability.

The Emotional Wheel™: A Tool to Help You Get and Stay in the Zone

The Emotional Wheel™ is a visual way to assess whether or not you are in the zone and able to do your best, and if not, to what degree your emotions are taking over and disrupting this ability. For this purpose, imagine your mind is a clock with 12 o'clock representing where you are in the zone. This is where you display your best cognitive ability, expertise, personality, and experience, making you an impactful leader. It is where you are calm, carefree of the outcome, and focused on the most important tasks at hand that are in your control.

You may have heard the term "flow state," which was recognized and named by Hungarian- American psychologist Mihaly Csikszentmihalyi, who wrote the national bestseller Flow. When you "flow," you are unaware of the past or future and solely focused on the task at hand. If you are presenting to your boss, you may be speaking slowly, enunciating, and focusing on the facts you are presenting. Your mind is free of past interactions that did not go well or of future catastrophes. What happens when we are unable to regulate our emotions and are, therefore, kicked out of the zone? What happens to our performance? Can we recover? How can we prepare and be emotionally agile to course correct? The Emotional Wheel™ is a tool to help you answer these questions, so you can have a measuring tool of sorts to test how your emotions are doing before, during, and after any important interaction.

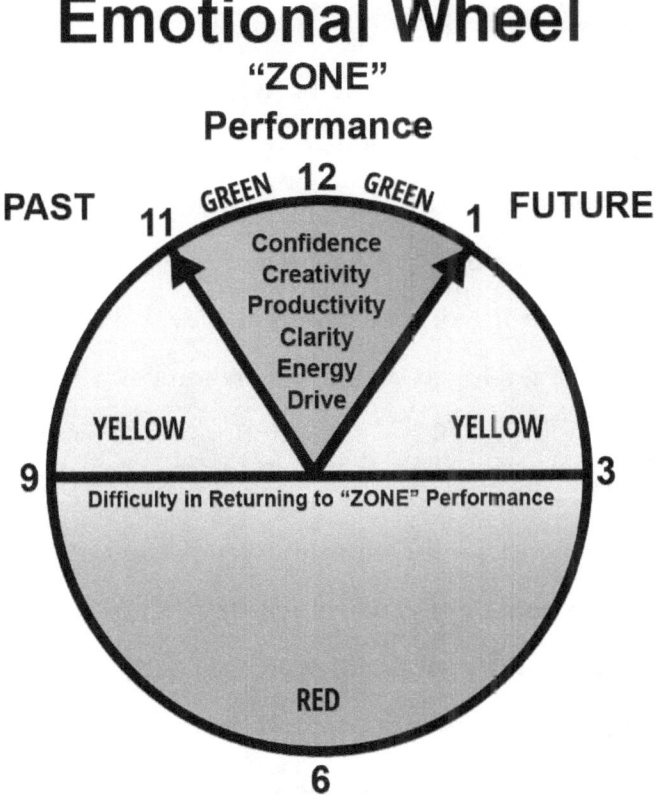

SHERYL KLINE, M.A. CHPC

The last time I was in Lake Forest, Illinois, visiting my best friend, Pam, I saw a couple of metal snow stakes while running along a trail. At the time, there was no snow. Sometimes in the winter and spring, you can see just the tip of the metal stakes poking out from the snow after a storm. Other times, after a big snowstorm, you can't see the snow stakes at all.

Since I was unfamiliar with the neighborhood, I depended on the snow stakes as markers to find my way around the trail and back to town. As long as I saw the marked stakes along the trail, even when other trails were introduced, or it wound a different way, I was calm, in the zone, and enjoying the run. When almost a mile passed without any snow stakes, my emotions were triggered, and I moved around the emotional wheel from the green, or the 12 o'clock zone, to deep into the yellow area. Where were they? More importantly, where was I? After 20 minutes of no snow stakes and various forks in the road, I was lost. Yes, emotions were running high. I have a high need for certainty, so the possibility of being lost was not ideal. I was approaching the red portion of the Emotional Wheel, which meant that I could not backtrack, think of familiar landmarks, or decide on the next best thing to do. The "what if" questions took over my brain. What if I'm lost (I was)? What if the temperature drops (it was)? What if, what if, what if until I thought of the Emotional Wheel™. I paused, took three deep breaths, noticed rather than experienced what I was feeling, and asked, "What's the best thing I can do right now?" This pause to take three breaths moved me from deep in the yellow back into the green or into the zone where I could take control of my next best step, which was to retrace my steps. Yes, I made it back to Pam's house in a reasonable time without any serious mishaps.

Let's say that I panicked, got stuck in fear, and was unable to think coherently and retrace my steps. I'm sure it would have eventually worked out, but perhaps I would have arrived home later and experienced the stress of being uncertain a little or a lot longer.

This example of an emotionally charged situation is not so different from finding an opportunity that scares you at first. If emotions begin to escalate, use the Emotional Wheel™ to assess where you are, and then you can use the A.D.D. Emotional Agility Blueprint™ to get back into the green zone. The Emotional Wheel™ is a gauge so you can be aware of where your zone performance is and so you can find the way toward your best performance when life has a surprise in store. It is the critical tool I've used throughout my years of coaching, helping world-class athletes, Olympians, and female executives to show up and deliver when the stakes are high.

But as human beings, while in the zone or in a flow state, we can succumb to thoughts about the past and the future. Remember the plane analogy I mentioned at the beginning of this book? Veering off course by just 1 percent may not seem like a big deal or major concern. However, if left unchecked, it worsens over time, eventually taking you somewhere you don't want to go.

The Emotional Wheel™ is not just a tool for the individual; it's a guide for teams and organizations so everyone is primed for the most productive time together. It's a shared language for emotional-state management, allowing groups to synchronize their most focused, collaborative, strategic, and congruent selves for collective effectiveness. Just as an orchestra tunes to a single pitch before a performance, teams align their emotional states to perform cohesively for the best outcome possible.

Biologically, What Happens During an Escalation?

From a biological perspective, one of our core needs is safety. Whether we are the ones who are lashing out, unable to control negative emotions, or we are the ones on the receiving end, we likely feel threatened, sending our Emotional Wheel™, reeling into past events or future what-ifs. Let's say our boss shuts down an idea and berates us for even suggesting it. We could feel unsafe and worried that we are not going to be seen in a favorable light going forward. It's never OK to be on the receiving end of a situation like this one, but we can use the Emotional Wheel™ to think through how to feel safe and respond in the best way possible.

An escalation, by definition, means to increase intensity. Due to our mirror neurons, our tendency to match our counterpart's emotions is extremely high. This is the case whether we are involved in an escalation or merely an observer. (BAI 2023). When we allow our emotions to match that of our counterpart, we pour fuel on the escalation fire until our interaction is doing more harm than good.

Let's look beyond the immediate team environment to the broader organizational culture. How does an organization embed emotional agility into its culture? The following are a couple of case studies of companies that have successfully integrated these principles, observing the impact on productivity, employee satisfaction, and overall corporate health.

Case Study: Technology Solutions—Janet's Software Success

Janet, the senior vice president of software development at a technology solutions company, faced the challenge of leading her team through the high- pressure launch of a new software product designed to streamline business operations.

Emotional Agility Application: Janet often found herself wrestling with anxiety and doubt, especially as launch deadlines approached. She implemented the Emotional Wheel strategy, consciously acknowledging these emotions but not letting them steer her decisions. Janet was the observer of her emotions without being the judge. She eventually learned how to make peace with her emotions. Though they used to short-circuit her ability to lead high-pressure meetings, she could now use them to fuel her ability to lead even more effectively when under pressure. Janet also learned how to make her team, and her leadership feel safe. Safe to speak up, safe to listen up, and safe to trust her.

Maintaining Focus: In team meetings, when discussions became heated, Janet practiced staying present, keeping her team present, and shifting her focus from fears of failure to immediate problem- solving, thus keeping her team zoned in on the current tasks.

Outcome: The software launch was successful, with fewer bugs than anticipated, largely due to Janet's ability to maintain emotional composure and lead her team with a clear, present mindset. Janet's boss also gave her the green light to launch her strategy and hire three more people.

When we think about a situation over and over in a very detailed way, using most or all of our senses, it can be extremely beneficial or extremely detrimental. The double blessing or double curse here is that emotions make experiences memorable, and our brain does not designate well between what we are thinking and what's actually happening (Hampton 2022). If we attach emotion to something that we'd like to improve and then think about it over and over, we are mentally practicing, becoming more proficient, and making what we desire more likely to happen. When our emotions are negative, or we catastrophize, what we believe to be true and our proficiency is powerfully impacted as well, only not in a good way.

In the next chapter, we'll combine a world-class tool with our Emotional Agility so we can accelerate our progress and become even more proficient in what matters most to us.

SHERYL KLINE, M.A. CHPC

CHAPTER 9

Visual Optimization

"Watch your thoughts; they become your words; watch your words, they become your actions; watch your actions, they become your habits; watch your habits, they become your character; watch your character, it becomes your destiny."-

— Ancient Chinese philosopher

Lao Tzu

You may be familiar with the term "visualization training." It's what high-level athletes like Olympians do to develop and refine their skills. There is prolific scientific research telling us that when mental rehearsal accompanies physical practice, athletes experience extraordinary results (Olympic Channel 2024).

Maybe you are not an Olympian, and you're wondering what visualization training has to do with your voice and impact in your role at work or in life. As it turns out a lot! This type of mental rehearsal is not reserved for the elite few. As a matter of fact, you are already quite good at it!

But for untrained visualization experts, this world-class tool tends to be used to our detriment rather than to our advantage.

Whenever we have a thought, opinion, or judgment about ourselves or others, we use visualization training. In other words, our ongoing thoughts can be like rehearsing a future triumph or catastrophizing a disaster that we don't want to happen. That is unless we know how to use visualization to our advantage.

Our thoughts also tend to shape our belief systems and actions; therefore, they can shape our destiny. Let's learn how to use this powerful tool the way Olympians do when maximizing their practice time and preparing for an important event. The events in your life are no less important, right?

Imagine an Olympian visualizing her routine countless times before the actual performance. Each twist, turn, and triumphant finish is etched into her neural pathways, making the imagined and the real indistinguishable in her mind. This mental preparation doesn't end with the vision of standing atop the podium and receiving a medal; it extends to every minute detail of practice, each drop of sweat, and every small triumph in the run-up to the event. The Olympian knows the texture of the grip tape, the resistance of the water, or the feel of the track beneath her feet. She's there, at the Olympics, every single day before she even arrives.

Visual optimization is not just about the end goal; it's about the process leading up to the end goal. It's about visualizing the steps, the incremental improvements, and the responses to various outcomes. Whether preparing for a crucial conversation or a pivotal presentation, visual optimization equips you to mentally rehearse and prime your mind and your body for success.

However, a common pitfall is the tendency toward negative visualization. This is where visualization can work against us rather than for us. We see the meeting going awry, the disapproving faces of our audience, or the disappointment in ourselves. This is not preparation; it is practicing the very thing that we so badly do not want to happen. We can overthink, making up stories in our minds about what others are thinking or how we might fall short. This was a familiar visualization script for me for many years until I understood the power of our thoughts to both lift us up and propel us forward or to stop us in our tracks and smack us down like a big wave crashing down on a novice surfer, crushing progress and self-efficacy along the way.

To effectively use visual optimization to uplift rather than diminish our dreams, let's learn to create and sustain a visual loop. This loop is a mental movie that we direct and star in—a movie that includes a beginning, a middle, and an end, focusing on aspects we can control. For example, when preparing to speak to executives, envision how you will start to command attention, how you will articulate your points with clarity, and how you will remain composed and factual throughout the discussion.

Let's further explore the concept of visual optimization and how to leverage it for peak performance in all areas of life. Visual optimization involves all senses; it's not solely the domain of sight. It includes the auditory roar of the crowd, the tactile feedback of your environment, and even the emotional atmosphere of your envisioned scenario. The more vividly you can engage all your senses, the more real the experience becomes in your mind, enhancing the neurological impact of the rehearsal.

But how do we build this visualization muscle to use for our benefit? Begin by setting the stage. Consider the environment you expect to be in. Is it a virtual meeting or in person? An intimate group or from a stage or big presentation?

How do you feel about what you're wearing? Are you standing tall? Visualize yourself as the confident, bold, and impactful leader you aspire to be in that moment. See yourself responding to certain obstacles, such as pushback or someone cutting you off, in a way that makes you proud of how you conduct yourself. In other words, spend your time thinking through how you would like an interaction to turn out rather than catastrophizing about what could go wrong. From there, we can reverse engineer how to get there. One way to do that is to create visual loops.

Visual Loops

Movies in the theater have a beginning, middle, and end. Characters and the plot are introduced, then there's the main story, and finally, the end of the movie. Visual loops are similar in that there is a beginning, middle, and end. When it comes to scripting what you will say or do to create your "mental movies," or visual loops, using as much detail as possible—including how you will feel, what smells you experience, and the expressions you will use—is key.

Let's say you are presenting a new idea to your boss for a project that is a bit unconventional but one that you believe wholeheartedly could have a tremendous impact on the business. You do not have control over how your boss will react or if you will gain her approval to move forward. What you do have control over is how you will prepare, beginning with your visual loop. If the meeting with your boss was a short movie consisting of the most important things

you have control over that will give you the best outcome possible, what would the beginning, middle, and end be? Perhaps the beginning would be pleasantries. You visualize smiling and expressing gratitude for her taking the time to meet. The middle part of the movie would be acknowledging shared goals and/or facts. You visualize saying, "It seems like our goal of increasing end customer use by 10 percent is front and center," and then sharing the research that supports your idea. The last part of the movie could be responding to three possible objections that she may have.

In order for your visual loop to be as real, lifelike, and memorable as possible, try attaching your other senses to it as well, not simply sight. For example, when your meeting is about to start, and you take a deep breath, what do you smell? Is it your favorite perfume, a cup of coffee, or the flowers at your desk? What do you hear? Are there birds chirping outside your window, the faint hum of your colleagues speaking outside of your office, or the crackle of a candle? Let's talk about taste. Did you just savor your morning g r e e n tea, have a very strong Altoid peppermint, or even imagine your favorite meal? Finally, how do you want to physically feel when you are running through your visual loop? Are you feeling excited, confident, strong, proud, happy, or relieved? As we've talked about earlier, emotions are a bit like glue. The stronger they are, the more they stick.

Most of us assign high levels of emotion to situations perceived as bad, such as getting fired, being told our idea is not viable, or being disregarded in a meeting. The minor to major accomplishments that are perceived as good often go unnoticed, such as a nod from your boss that you're doing a good job, finishing a project that's been tough, or a smile from our kids. While this is 100 percent normal and completely understandable, maybe it's time to flip the switch on our emotional responses to these situations!

For the not-so-good, give yourself permission to feel what you feel: anger, fear, frustration, and so on. Honor those feelings and decide when you are ready to neutralize the negative. Remember the A.D.D Emotional Agility Blueprint?

Raise Awareness, Distance from the emotion by saying "I notice" rather than "I am," and then Decide how you visualize yourself moving forward.

For the great situations, big and small, visualize as if your best friend just shared the good news. How would you respond if she said her boss gave her a thumbs up on a project that was difficult, that she finished the project, or that her teenager, who's been aloof for months, has finally asked to spend time with her? Express the same compassion, caring, and excitement for yourself as you would for a dear friend.

This is how you'll loosen the hold of emotions that do not serve you and strengthen the ones that do. If the visual loops available to you were like books on a shelf, you would be better equipped to organize the library in your favor so that you can draw on resources that will accelerate your progress rather than hinder your greatness.

Reflection:

What could a visual loop or mental movie for an upcoming conversation or presentation look like for you? For example, a strong handshake, focus on facts, and eye contact.

SHERYL KLINE, M.A. CHPC

Beginning:

_____

_____

_____

Middle:

_____

_____

_____

End:

_____

_____

_____

The Emotional Wheel, introduced in the previous section, also plays a role in visual optimization. It helps us navigate our emotional responses as we visualize different outcomes. We may catch ourselves beginning a negative visual loop and moving from our zone performance in the green to the yellow or even the red. We can notice the emotion, hold up an imaginary stop sign, thank the emotion, and let it know that it no longer serves us. The internal monologue for this might be something like, "I notice I am feeling so worried. Stop right here. Thank you for this feeling of worry, for there is wisdom in it. I release this worry because it no longer serves me or is helpful."

By staying zoned in, we ensure that our visual loops, the mental rehearsals we practice, are positive and constructive, not fear-based or negative.

It is also important to balance visual optimization with physical practice. While mental rehearsal is powerful and can have a positive effect even if we don't physically practice, it is most effective when combined with actual practice (Brouziyne & Molinaro, 2005). For example, if you have a meeting coming up with your boss, run through your visual loop five to 10 times or until you feel proficient, and then ask a family member, friend, or colleague to role-play as your boss. If this is not possible, physically practicing in the space where your meeting will be or somewhere similar can be helpful, too. Just do your best to combine your visualization practice with physical practice that is as close to the environment you'll be in when it's game time. This helps to create a sense of familiarity, competence, and safety if you choose to think of your counterpart as entering your space rather than you treading lightly on his or hers.

A Tool for Life

Visual optimization is not restricted to professional settings. How can we use this tool to enhance our personal lives? Whether it's visualizing a difficult conversation with a loved one or mentally rehearsing a personal goal, the principles of visual optimization apply. We get to choose what we rehearse in our mind, what we become more proficient in, what we believe, and how our performance will guide our reality of what unfolds. Let's say we want to decrease our body fat by 8 percent, and one of our main movement strategies is to increase weight training to three times a week. We get to decide what our visual loop is.

Is it positive and empowering?

Beginning: Gym clothes on

Middle: Taking group weight-training classes I like

End: High fiving my instructor or a fellow classmate at the end

Or is it negative and disempowering?

Beginning: Frustrated looking in the mirror

Middle: Feeling hopeless

End: Going back to bed

Remember, our brains do not designate well between thinking something over and over and actually doing it if we are using strong emotional signals (Saplakoglu, 2023), so it is important to choose our thoughts wisely!

The (Unfortunate) Power of Ruminating According to the Merriam-Webster dictionary, ruminating has two definitions:

1. The act or process of regurgitating and chewing again previously swallowed food

2. Obsessive thinking about an idea, situation, or choice, especially when it interferes with normal mental functioning

Most of us, at one time or another have either regurgitated an event repeatedly, even when we know it's not in our best interest. Maybe it's when we received a suboptimal performance review from our boss, when a friend was insensitive, or when our partner did something that was upsetting. Around the Emotional Wheel™ we go, pouring more emotional fuel onto something that was unpleasant or hurtful until we are deep in the yellow or even in the red.

When we are in a highly emotional state, our brains are aroused, neurotransmitters are firing, and the details that we perceive as important are much more memorable than the memories that are mundane, repetitive, or commonplace. This is for good reason! From an evolutionary standpoint, one reason is to protect us from danger. If we saw a saber-toothed tiger just around the corner, it would be a good idea to remember when and where we saw it to protect ourselves in the future. If we were walking along that same path, but it was peaceful without any threats, we would be less likely to notice and remember a specific color, a flower, or a unique tree that could put us on high alert. A more present-day example might be a time when we spoke up in a meeting, and our idea was dismissed as trivial or not relevant. This may not put our life in danger like it was with the saber-toothed tiger, but we may feel a similar emotional threat, "You are not safe to speak up."

According to the Healthline article, Emotions Can Affect Your Memory: Here's Why and How to Handle It, from a neurological standpoint, emotional events are easier to remember (Swaim, 2022). This is because highly charged emotions activate our small but mighty emotion-processing-focused part of our brain and the part of our brain that is responsible for transferring short-term memories to long-term memories at almost exactly the same time. This process helps us to store memories more effectively (Tyng, Amin, Saad, Malik 2017).

If we ruminate or create visual loops that are charged with negative emotion and then play them over and over again, we can hijack the conversation, presentation, or meeting in our mind before it even begins and continue on long after it ends. The ADD Emotional Agility Blueprint was introduced as a tool to prepare for interactions with others, but it can also be used for yourself when you notice your Emotional Wheel™ is starting to spin. Raise awareness and create distance ("I notice I'm feeling XYZ when ABC happens.") Then decide ("The best thing for me to do right now that I have control over is XYZ.").

This could be to take a breath, step outside, refocus on the facts, etc.

Building this type of mental resilience is a safety net that catches us when our thoughts get derailed toward the negative. It helps us to avoid a possible wreck where our emotions hijack our ability to think and be our best. Visual loops that are negatively charged and repeated are effective, but not in a good way, and can be highly damaging and distracting. The reason being that we are practicing the very thing that we do not want to happen, leading us toward a self-fulfilling prophecy. Visual loops are a weapon for your toolbelt. Just be sure to use them for your benefit!

Visual optimization can be used in group settings as well. Teams use collective visualization to align their goals and strategies. Group exercises can help teams to synchronize their visualizations and enhance team cohesion and performance.

Additionally, the Emotional Wheel's principles can be integrated into visual optimization to manage the emotions that arise during visualization. It's important to be mindful of our emotions during visualization, ensuring that our visualizations are not derailed by fear or anxiety but are instead empowered by positivity and a focus on success. Let's see how a few women used visual optimization to influence their belief system their actions, and eventually to bring their visions to life.

Case Study: Architectural Firm Revitalization— Pam's Sustainable Designs

Pam, the director of an established architectural firm, faced the ambitious task of integrating sustainable practices into all her company's projects. She envisioned creating buildings that were not only aesthetically pleasing but also environmentally responsible.

Visual Optimization: Pam spent mornings visualizing her designs, transforming city skylines, and being featured in top architectural magazines, focusing on the ripple effect of sustainability in urban development.

Mental Rehearsals: She meticulously rehearsed client presentations, visualizing herself articulating the benefits of sustainable design and its long-term ROI, convincing clients to embrace greener buildings.

Optimism in Visualization: Maintaining a positive outlook, Pam envisaged her firm becoming an industry leader in eco-friendly design, setting a new standard for future constructions.

Outcome: Pam's dedication to visual optimization paid off as her firm secured several high- profile contracts, leading to awards and recognition as pioneers in sustainable architecture.

Case Study: Culinary Arts Expansion—Isabella's Organic Restaurant Chain

Isabella, an acclaimed chef and restaurateur, aimed to expand her small organic eatery into a nationwide restaurant chain that emphasized locally sourced and organic ingredients.

Visual Optimization: She imagined diners in multiple cities enjoying her farm-to-table dishes, appreciating the depth of flavor and nutritional value, and becoming regular patrons. **Mental Rehearsals:** Isabella practiced her pitch to potential investors, envisioning their enthusiasm as they tasted her signature dishes and comprehended her vision for organic dining.

Optimism in Visualization: With an optimistic mindset, she foresaw her restaurant chain, sparking a larger movement toward sustainable eating practices across the country.

Outcome: Isabella's clear vision and positive visualizations attracted investors and customers alike, leading to a successful expansion and a burgeoning movement towards healthier, sustainable eating habits.

Case Study: Automotive Industry Shift—Lara's Electric Vehicle Initiative

Lara, an executive vice president of corporate strategy at a midsize car manufacturing company, was determined to steer the company toward electric vehicles (EVs). Her goal was to contribute to reducing carbon emissions and revolutionize the market with affordable EVs.

Visual Optimization: Lara visualized her company's new line of EVs becoming the go-to choice for eco-conscious consumers, with long lines of customers waiting at dealerships on launch day.

Mental Rehearsals: She rehearsed engineering meetings and investor briefings, seeing herself confidently presenting technological innovations and the positive environmental impact.

Optimism in Visualization: Keeping a positive vision, Lara saw her company receiving accolades for its contributions to green technology and becoming a household name in the EV market.

Outcome: Lara's un w av e r i n g o pti mi sm and strategic visualization led to the successful launch.

You now know more about how to harness a tool that you've already been using for most of your life. Visualization has the power to uplift or the power to dismantle dreams and aspirations. Do not expect to make a 180-degree shift to always being optimistic and positive. Be compassionate as you begin to raise your awareness of visual loops that are not helpful so you can begin to guide yourself back to the visual loops that will help move you forward toward the best and most successful version of you. Again, "be the observer and not the judge." Notice when you may be ruminating or in a negative loop and be curious about it. "There it is again!" You can then ask, "What visual loop might be more helpful?"

I was recently driving in the car with my daughter along the Pacific Coast Highway in Cardiff- by-the-Sea, California. She was telling me about a wedding she saw on the beach and how the couple was so cute and "looked so in love." She then told me that she began thinking she may never find that type of deep love. The more she thought about it, the more emotional and sadder she became. I had to catch myself from saying, "You are beautiful. You will find that special person. He'll be so lucky …" which disregarded what was weighing heavy on her heart and her unspoken plea for me to just listen, not fix.

Eventually, I said, "Do you know with absolute certainty that what you are saying is true, that you will never find lasting, deep, and compassionate love?" She said, "No, I am not certain."

I went on, "When you see the couple getting married on the beach, could you imagine what it might be like to feel that type of love, the joy, fun, and adventure that you're looking for? What would the first date feel like? Introducing him to your friends and family? Then, knowing he was the one that you'd like to spend the rest of your life with?" Finally, I asked, "What is something fun to do this weekend where you might meet new friends that have similar values and interests?"

She has learned how to gently guide or nudge her thoughts from a negative loop to a more positive and optimistic one. From here she is creating a plan for what she'll need to learn about herself to be able to be open to receiving this type of love.

Whether you're looking for love or looking to receive a raise, a new role, or to gain buy-in on a new initiative, creating positive and helpful visual loops will help you create the reality that you are looking for. However, as one of my mentors, Chris Voss says, "You've got to get in your reps." Confidence is built by mental strength, such as emotional agility, internal monologue, and visualization, but it's also built by rolling up your sleeves and putting in the work.

SHERYL KLINE, M.A. CHPC

SHERYL KLINE, M.A. CHPC

C H A P T E R   1 0

Practice

At a recent conference, Pat sat in the audience as her senior vice president was on stage delivering a keynote for their cybersecurity company. Pat marveled at how her SVP stood on stage with confidence and how she commanded full and unwavering attention from the audience. Pat, a brilliant but introverted rising leader, knew she needed to get more confident on stage. As she watched her SVP get a standing ovation, she was certain that her SVP was born with poise and confidence.

Pat's assumption could not be further from the truth. Just like we do not acquire ideal fitness without consistent work moving our body, we are not innately born with world-class levels of confidence and stage presence either. Confidence is impacted by many things that are not in our control, including but not limited to how we were raised and our past experiences, for better or worse.

In addition to how we speak to ourselves (internal voice), regulate our emotions (emotional agility), and use our thoughts to become more proficient (visual optimization), there is another tool that we have control over, which can lead to greater confidence, and that's practice.

As we become more competent by practicing, we tend to become more confident (Eikenberry, 2022). As you can imagine or possibly have experienced, building confidence without feeling competent is a trick that we play on ourselves that rarely, if ever, works. Practice is not simply repetitive action but a deliberate introspective effort to identify gaps in your skillset and work diligently to bridge them, according to Dr. Anders Ericsson, a prolific researcher on the science of expertise and author of the best-selling book *Peak*.

Practice is the cornerstone of confidence. It's the steady drumbeat to which the march of progress advances, and those who commit to it are the ones who often appear lucky to the outside world. From my personal experience working with world-class athletes and dozens of prolific and influential female executives and the insights I've gained from my mentors, I've come to understand the transformative power of disciplined practice.

Bo Eason, a mentor of mine, is a testament to the philosophy that dedicated effort leads to extraordinary results.

Bo's transition from an NFL safety to a Broadway playwright wasn't a stroke of luck; it was the culmination of relentless practice, a journey fraught with setbacks yet driven by an unwavering belief in possibility. His career-ending injury could have been a full stop, but for Bo, it was merely a comma in the narrative of his life. He envisioned a new dream and pursued it with the tenacity and fervor that characterized his time on the football field. His story is a powerful reminder that the path to achieving the exceptional is paved with far more effort than many are willing to invest.

Similarly, another mentor who has influenced my perspective is Brendon Burchard. Brendon encapsulates the idea of the "confidence competence loop," an insightful concept that illustrates the cyclical nature of learning and growth. As we acquire new skills and knowledge, our burgeoning competence fuels our confidence, encouraging us to stretch further to reach higher. This loop is the engine of personal development, but it's fueled by the gritty, often monotonous work of daily practice. It's the repetitive drills, the conscious refinement, and the incremental improvements that eventually lead to leaps in capability and achievement.

Whether a thought leader, Olympic athlete, or anyone else who has achieved greatness, it's the consistent practice that is done long before the curtain rises, or the competition begins that champions confidence. Many times, it's those who are best in the world at what they do who arrive early, practice more than everyone else, or who are most consistent with the effort they put in to hone their performance.

Reflection:

For a recent past interaction or an upcoming one, what's one thing to level up your practice so you feel more confident?

Consistency and Accountability Are Key

Practicing consistently, with focus and determination, is not without its challenges. The road is long, the work can be tedious, and the progress is sometimes imperceptible. It's here that most falter, where the grittiness required to persevere is lacking. This is where understanding the concept of blind spots becomes crucial. To stay on track, we must be acutely aware of and open to recognizing these blind spots— areas where we may be self-sabotaging without even realizing it, placing an invisible wall up to protect ourselves from trying. Human nature tends toward comfort and ease, but growth requires the opposite. This is why incorporating accountability into one's practice regimen is a strategy employed by the most successful individuals. Accountability keeps us honest, pushes us beyond our comfort zones, and ensures that the commitment to practice doesn't wane when enthusiasm dips. It helps us keep our promises to ourselves.

Choosing an accountability partner can help you show up for the small and sometimes mundane tasks that propel you forward, inch by inch. This is someone who not only understands and supports your aspirations but is also willing to challenge you and call you out when you falter. This person isn't merely a cheerleader; they are a coach and confidant, instrumental in ensuring that you don't veer off the path of disciplined practice.

With an accountability partner, you share not just victories but also the strategies that led to those wins. Celebrate the process goals—those you have direct control over—and share the weekly triumphs, no matter how small they may seem. These celebrations are affirmations of your commitment and consistency, reinforcing the positive loop between confidence and competence.

However, imperfection is part of the human condition, and there will be times when you fall short of your commitments. Here, the role of your accountability partner is to help you navigate back to the course. You commit to owning your shortcomings and devising a plan to improve. This candid sharing fosters a climate of trust and mutual growth.

Course corrections are an integral part of the practice journey. When things go awry, when the practice falters, or when unexpected challenges arise, we must be agile enough to adjust our strategies. This agility keeps you moving forward, allowing you to view each setback not as a failure but as an opportunity to learn and evolve.

It's important to remember that many of the greatest successes have arisen from past failures. If it were not for failures, some of the most well-known inventions may never have come to exist. Everything from sticky notes, the implantable pacemaker, and microwave ovens to Velcro and Super Glue were born from failed attempts to make something else. (Diversified Spaces 2021.) The key is to have some grace with yourself, try to improve, and keep going. When you encounter obstacles, it's not about self-reproach but about recalibrating your approach. If a particular method or strategy isn't yielding the desired results, then it's time for a tactical shift. This might involve seeking additional resources, soliciting feedback, or simply changing your practice routine to rekindle momentum.

In your discussions with your accountability partner, it's essential to detail how you'll approach these course corrections. For instance, if a project isn't advancing as swiftly as you'd hoped, consider implementing focused work sessions or seeking mentorship to enhance your effectiveness.

Now, to truly grasp the essence of practice and its role in doing the small yet consistent things that lead to the results you're looking for, let's explore the five foundational elements that contribute to an effective practice routine. These form the bedrock upon which skill, mastery, and, eventually, confidence is built.

The first element is consistency. Practice is not an occasional endeavor; it's a daily commitment. It's the quiet dedication that accumulates over time into expertise. Each session, no matter how small, contributes to the larger picture of progress. Consistency turns practice into habit and habit into second nature. We typically do not receive any awards or recognition for practice. It's not glamorous and often not even fun or enjoyable. Consistency is when my tennis player son hits 100 serves alone on the court before school every day when he would prefer to play a game. Consistency is the 300 to 500 shots NBA star Steph Curry takes after team practice and his teammates have left the court. Our practice, such as working on the tone and cadence of our words or rehearsing a presentation, may not be this rigorous, but it is no less important.

The second element is intentionality. Each practice session should have a clear focus. What specific skill or aspect are you working on? What outcome do you wish to achieve in this session? Intentionality ensures that your practice is purposeful and directed, maximizing the efficiency of your efforts.

The third element is reflection. After each practice session, take time to reflect on what went well, what didn't, and why. Reflection transforms experiences into insights and cements learning. It allows you to adjust your approach and refine your techniques based on concrete feedback.

The fourth element is challenge. Practice should push you beyond your current limits. It should be difficult enough to stretch your abilities but not so challenging that it becomes discouraging. Finding the right level of challenge is crucial for growth and prevents complacency. For example, if you tend to be low emotion and direct like me, what would it look like to take your energy up a notch, ask one more question while listening intently, and stand a little taller when entering a room?

The fifth element is measurability. Set benchmarks and goals within your practice that allow you to track progress. Whether it's a time goal, a quality standard, or a productivity measure, having tangible metrics will help you see the fruits of your labor and can be incredibly motivating.

Practice is where the seeds of potential are nurtured. It's where dreams take shape into reality through the relentless pursuit of improvement. Repetition and deliberate effort physically alter our brain structure, enhancing neural connections and making certain actions feel more natural and less cognitively demanding.

It is through practice that we come to realize that we are not bound by our current abilities but are always capable of improving regardless of our current circumstances.

To aid in your practice routine on your journey to becoming more confident, try using this Momentum Builder™

worksheet, which is an accountability structure to make practice more consistent and more enjoyable.

Momentum Builder Worksheet

Accountability Partner: Choose someone who will show up and challenge and support you on your march toward what's next for you.

Who will yours be?

_____

_____

_____

Declaration: What is your long-term objective that you will declare to yourself and to your accountability partner? You can refer to your Success Roadmap, where your Long-Term Objective should be listed.

What's your declaration?

I declare that I will:

_____

_____

_____

Share: Create the time and space to share your declaration as well as your consistent progress with your accountability partner. This could be a family member, friend, or colleague. It's important that he or she is someone who will show up for you, has your best interest at heart, and is willing to challenge you.

When will you connect with your accountability buddy for your declaration and for consistent check- ins?

_____

_____

_____

Celebration: How and when will you reward yourself and celebrate your progress?

I will celebrate accomplishing _ by _:

_____

_____

_____

Course Corrections: What did I learn, and how can I recommit and get back on track?

I learned that _ and one thing I can do to get back on track is _:

_____

_____

_____

Case Study: Tech Innovation—Alisha's Coding Bootcamp Breakthrough

Alisha, the chief information officer of a pioneering software development firm, faced the challenge of upskilling her team with the latest programming languages. Despite a tight budget, she needed to practice what she preached about continuous learning and innovation.

Deliberate Practice: Alisha initiated a series of in-house coding boot camps. She led the first sessions herself, showing her commitment to hands-on learning and growth.

Accountability Partner: She paired up senior developers with juniors, establishing a mentorship program that fostered a culture of mutual accountability and support.

Consequences and Corrections: Alisha set clear milestones for skill acquisition, with time allocated for peer reviews. When progress stalled, she arranged hackathons to reignite enthusiasm and practical application of new skills.

Result: Alisha's approach led to a surge in team competence, significantly reducing the learning curve for new technologies. The company gained a reputation for being at the cutting edge, attracting both clients and talent.

Case Study: Finance Sector—Beatriz's Investment Strategy Reinvention

Beatriz, an ambitious senior hedge fund manager, aimed to shift her team's approach from traditional to more innovative, data-driven investment strategies. Skepticism was rife, and Beatriz knew she needed to embody the change.

Deliberate Practice: She dedicated the first hour of her day to studying emerging markets and new analysis software, setting a standard for her team.

Accountability Partner: Beatriz worked closely with the analytics team to set realistic key performance indicators (KPIs) for adopting new strategies, ensuring her progress was transparent and measurable.

Consequences and Corrections: If a new strategy underperformed, Beatriz encouraged her team to present a case study on the learnings rather than focus on the setback, fostering a growth mindset.

Result: The fund began outperforming competitors as Beatriz's team embraced data analytics, leading to higher returns and industry accolades for innovation.

Case Study: Retail Expansion—Claudia's Global Brand Launch

Claudia, the ambitious senior vice president of operations at a fashion retail chain, was tasked with expanding the brand globally. She faced cultural nuances and varying consumer behaviors in new markets.

Deliberate Practice: Claudia conducted market research trips, personally engaging with local consumers and businesses to understand each market's unique needs.

Accountability Partner: She established a cross-functional team from various departments to synchronize the expansion efforts and hold each other accountable.

Consequences and Corrections: Whenever a market entry did not meet projections, Claudia led a retrospective analysis, adjusting the approach with input from local teams to better tailor the brand's presence.

Result: Claudia's focused practice approach resulted in successful market entries, with localized strategies increasing brand acceptance and profitability abroad.

How to Keep Up the Great Work

Part of building confidence is creating a workflow that is sustainable. If you are already a high performer, which I imagine you are, your success up to this point may have come at a price. Maybe the currency you've paid is time, working beyond typical work hours. Perhaps it's availability, being contacted and constantly interrupted many times a day in a multitude of ways. Maybe the price is stress or other impacts on your health. Confidence is not only a tool to be used for your next level at work, to dream bigger, to have crucial conversations, and to have your voice heard. Confidence is a companion you will need by your side to speak up about what you need what's not working, and to propose changes you'd like to make.

If your boss, your team, and even your family are used to you being accessible at a moment's notice to answer questions, put out fires, help when they are struggling, and attend to their non emergencies, they may react to your new boundaries or accessibility. For you to have the greatest impact while operating in your zone of genius, you will need the confidence to raise your awareness of what you need to sustain your progress and success. Most importantly, you will need confidence to ask for it. The consequences of existing in a status quo that is not sustainable are overwhelming. When overwhelmed, our productivity, innovative ability, profitability, and ability to have an impact can be hindered. It's not only costly for us but also costly to our companies.

According to a 2023 Gallup study, that figure is approximately $1.9 trillion.

Let's have a look at what it means to be overwhelmed, how it's experienced in our bodies, and how to build the confidence to decide what we need to manage to feel overwhelmed and sustain our impact.

Managing Overwhelm

In a coaching session with Becky (not her real name), an executive vice president of a technology company, she told me that she felt like her job consumed her. While she checked in with friends via text, she had not seen the few women who were her confidants and safe space to feel the ups and downs of life. There was no time. Travel ramped up again after COVID, the pressure to grow the business was elevated, and there was tremendous pressure on her and her team. Becky was all too familiar with the feeling of sprinting in a race that had no end in sight. While she loved what she did, Becky was tired and uncertain if she could sustain the pace or if she even wanted to.

When we feel overwhelmed, we don't feel safe. Perhaps we feel like our job is threatened if we don't get an insurmountable amount of work done if we don't hit our numbers, if a project goes wrong, or if we lose a big customer. Whether a perceived or real threat, it's real to us. Feeling overwhelmed can trigger our fight-or-flight response to an event that feels like a crisis, or it can be a low-volume hum in the back of our mind that is a thief of our energy and motivation.

If we're experiencing a fight-or-flight response, a chain of reactions can result in an increased heart rate, blood pressure, and breathing rate. Our bodies can stay in fight-or-flight mode for 20 to 60 minutes after the threat is gone, which is how long it takes for the parasympathetic nervous system to return to pre-arousal levels. (Cherry 2024). From an evolutionary perspective, during a fight-or-flight response, we prepare to fight to save our lives or to run away from danger. Our blood flow is directed from our brain to our muscles, so we can either fight the sabertoothed tiger or run away from it. Neither seems like a great option!

With diminished blood flow to the most developed part of our brain, the cerebral cortex, along with a host of other physiological factors, it is no wonder why we are unable to remember what to say.

We might say something we regret, or we fail to innovate a new or better solution in this state.

Even with world-class tools to regulate emotions, feeling overwhelmed can disable our best performance and our team's best performance and seep into our company culture. Left unchecked, feeling overwhelmed and emotionally dysregulated is like riding a runaway train that keeps taking us further and faster off track. Emotional agility and staying in or reacclimating to the green zone is what will help you, your team, and your organization course correct, and get back to accessing your best work.

Being overwhelmed is rooted in the feeling of lacking control. We lack control over what's expected and if we'll be able to deliver results that will ensure we are safe in our role. In an era marked by unprecedented disruption, it's vital to take a moment to breathe—to reflect, to look ahead, and to reclaim a semblance of control. This breath is more than a pause; it's an opportunity to recalibrate our strategies and recover from the onslaught of overwhelming feelings that can stifle our joy productivity, and, ultimately, the profitability of our company.

Your hard work has undoubtedly carved the path to your current success, but it's essential to recognize that lingering in a state of overwhelm can precipitate declines in all facets of our lives, affecting not only us but also our team, our loved ones, and our larger community. The ripple effects of a leader's stress are profound and far-reaching.

Elevating your team to embody sustainable high performance can have a transformative impact on your organization. As CEO and founder of The Zone Lab, I've had the privilege of guiding leaders from prestigious companies through this journey of self- realization and strategic execution. My clients from Google Ventures, Microsoft, Pixar, and Bank of America, among others, have all experienced the profound benefits of this focused approach.

As we look to confront and navigate through the fog of feeling overwhelmed, it's critical to arm ourselves with tools for emotional agility and boundaries. These tools tried and tested within Fortune 100 and 500 companies, are not merely theoretical concepts but practical instruments designed for immediate application.

Let's first establish the groundwork for success. Let's say you hire a fitness coach who is also well-versed in nutrition.

She would not begin by stocking your pantry with sweets, crackers, or unhealthy food choices. Similarly, we must clear any obstacles that could impede the team's path to success. This preparatory stage involves ensuring alignment across all levels of your organization.

When and how are you available? Are communication tools like Microsoft Teams, Slack, instant messages, emails, etc., interrupting you constantly with other people's emergencies? When do notifications go on and off? Is your calendar accessible to others? If so, when can you block out time, and is that blocked time respected? How much of your day is consumed by meetings? How much time do you have to do your actual work?

If you are nodding right now because one or more of these questions rings all too true, let's take a baby step in another direction. Let's list one work and one personal boundary you can begin implementing immediately to reduce the feeling of overwhelm and support your ability to be your best:

Reflection:

One boundary I can recommend or request setting at work so I can be more productive and feel less overwhelmed is:

_____

_____

_____

I'll begin by implementing this or bring it up with my boss or team on (date):

_____

_____

_____

This is important to me and is a win for myself, my team, and my company because:

_____

_____

_____

One boundary I can suggest setting at home, so I'll feel more calm and less overwhelmed is:

_____

_____

_____

I'll bring it up with my partner/family on (date/time):

_____

_____

_____

This is a win for myself and my family because:

_____

_____

_____

Managing overwhelming feelings begins with you deciding how you would like to feel. Then, you get to reverse-engineer the steps to make it happen. Granted, there are many factors that you do not have control over, but you do have control over how you perceive your environment as well as the most important steps you can take to create boundaries for your sustainable success. Once you have this clarity on how you would like to feel and the boundaries you'd like to have, take the baby steps you do have control over while you're making broader strides toward your goal. For example, block 30 minutes before you log on to go over a course you've started or to get a head start on a project. Better yet, wake up a few minutes earlier to walk, meditate, and/or journal.

Reflection:

When is a good way for me to create time or reclaim time that is mine, and what would I like to use it for so I can feel calmer and in control?

_____

_____

_____

Now that you've homed in on your Clarity for what's next created a Success Roadmap to get there, and gained the Confidence to see your roadmap through, let's make sure you can gain buy-in from those who can champion your efforts and get behind your asks. Whether you are in the first couple years of your career or are a seasoned executive, being highly influential is how your ideas, impact, and sustainability will gain traction and be amplified.

SHERYL KLINE, M.A. CHPC

SECTION 3

Influence:
How to Mobilize Allies

Have you ever found yourself in a salary negotiation, interview, important customer meeting, or initiative push and felt like it was not going well? Maybe in the pit of your stomach, you felt like you were losing ground like the other person was stepping away or disengaging. Perhaps you felt like you'd have to make unanticipated compromises or felt afraid to push too hard for what you want and truly feel you deserve. It's safe to say that most of us have been in one of these predicaments before.

In order to speak up, be heard, and have the greatest voice and impact, it's important to know how to inspire others to get behind your efforts and your asks. Even if you already consider yourself influential with your peers and subordinates, are you with your boss and the rest of your leadership team? Understandably, speaking to leadership can be intimidating and cause us to stay quiet when we have something important to say. On your leadership journey, let's make sure you not only have a seat at the table but a strong and well-respected voice at the table as well, especially with your leadership and peers.

Whether your goal is money, stock options, nonpecuniary gains, or the dignity of having your voice heard, valued, and respected, learning how to be highly influential, especially with those in power, is a priceless tool. With influence you can have the contribution and impact you want and deserve.

Sarah (not her real name), for example, was far from unique when she was referred to me for coaching after an initial salary conversation with her boss. Despite her best efforts, the first conversation with her boss took a nosedive, along with Sarah's ability to stay calm and optimistic. She noticed that her frustration mounted with each passing minute of the conversation, which was supposed to be a predictable celebration of her success.

Sarah knew the expected increase range for this role was between six and eight percent. Based on performance reviews and the information she had from colleagues, she was confident she'd be close to, if not at, eight percent. Possibly due to a company restructuring and a tight budget, her salary increase came in at only 5.8 percent, which depleted the excitement she was feeling going into the meeting. What made this not- great news even worse was her boss's demeanor, which lacked any compassion, camaraderie. or interest in fighting for her.

During the conversation, Sarah's thoughts went from optimistic to disappointed to disbelief, causing her to get a bit defensive and thrown off her game. Her boss then sounded irritated and lashed out, exclaiming that her request was unacceptable, especially due to their current budget constraints. All of her preparedness faltered because the emotion she was experiencing was distracting her. She began defending her values and what she was asking for until her boss ended the meeting, saying, "That's the best I can do."

Prepared But Not Prepared Enough

Sarah felt that she was well-prepared and had a great case, making her boss's decision to give her the expected raise an easy one. Her successes and those of her team were well documented, and her performance plans over the past year were stellar. She had also done the research to know that her raise was not a big ask and well within the range of others who had her new title. Despite her track record and conservative ask, Sarah was still receiving pushback.

But why? Sarah was worthy and deserving and had done her homework to support and defend her salary request.

What she was missing, which is missing from many people's dashboards, was world-class mental and tactical preparation.

The reason why Sarah was prepared but not prepared enough was twofold and pivotal in understanding where Sarah—and many others in her position—often stumble. First, it's essential to recognize the role that mental preparation plays in professional settings. While passion and determination are lauded, negative emotions like anger can be detrimental, especially for women. Groundbreaking research from the National Institute of Health has shed light on how women's expressions of anger in the workplace can lead to negative evaluations of their competence and status. Unfortunately, this double standard often penalizes women for the same emotional expressions that can lead to men being rewarded (Parsons 2007).

Sarah's frustration, while entirely justified, was not going to secure her the salary she sought. This wasn't just unfair—it was indicative of a broader systemic issue that could not be remedied overnight. However, the immediate goal was not to reform the system but to navigate it successfully to achieve Sarah's objective: the raise she deserved.

The second critical oversight in Sarah's preparation was that she was deeply invested in her narrative, her qualifications, her contributions, and her perceived value. Of course, this is important to verbalize, but it's not what to communicate first. What about her boss's perspective? Sarah did not step out of her own shoes and into her managers to understand his perspective, his constraints, the stress he was under, and his motivations. What would make him look favorable to his leadership? What was important to him? What would make his job easier?

Influence is not about convincing others of our worth, the importance of our voice, or that what we are asking is valid. Influence is about creating trust and safety prior to making an ask, like approaching a frightened stray dog with food. Until it feels safe and trusts us, we cannot bring it close enough to be helpful. When we make an ask or try to gain buy-in without establishing trust and safety first, we run the risk of being perceived as a threat. Making an ask before understanding and validating the other person's condition, whether you like them or respect them, is premature. It's like walking up to that dog with a leash and demanding her to come over to you.

Physiological safety is one of our most basic biological needs. (McCloud 2024.) In a work context, this could mean the safety related to keeping our job so we can keep a roof over our heads and provide for ourselves and our families. This may be a very real concern for us, but it could also be a real concern for our boss or whomever we are trying to influence. Building influence does not start with what you want, what you feel you deserve, or why you are asking.

Building Influence starts with the other person. Once Sarah shifted her approach, connecting and demonstrating understanding and caring for her boss, the dynamic changed. For their next meeting, she took a step back, stood in her boss's shoes, and prepared as if she were her manager, understanding his priorities, pressures, and the language that resonated with him. This pivot was the key to unlocking the conversation and steering it toward a mutually beneficial outcome.

In Sarah's second attempt, armed with a new strategy and a deeper understanding of the subtleties of influence, she not only secured her raise but exceeded her own expectations. Instead of leading the conversation with herself, Sarah got her boss's attention by first connecting with him and what he might be experiencing. She initially thought her boss's primary concern was growing revenue in the short term. It turned out her perception of his situation was wrong, but he was grateful for her acknowledgment of his perspective and glad to fill in the gaps. Never worry about being a little off when leading a conversation with empathy, as most people will gladly correct you, giving you more information and insight, which will come in handy later. Sarah's boss told her that while growing revenue was important in the near term, what was most important was putting the pieces in place for a long-term strategy. This was very important information to know when Sarah went on to frame up her ask for the second time.

Whether in a salary negotiation, an important interview, or a critical meeting, becoming highly influential is a staple of a powerful personal and professional life. There is a process to follow prior to making an ask of someone else. Without following this process, our ask can fall short or do more harm than good. It can seem premature or off-putting. Making an ask, especially one that is significant or requires a lot of the other person/people prior to creating trust, acknowledgment, and, therefore, the safety that comes along with knowing you are working toward a common goal, is similar to asking someone to marry you after the first date. It's strange, will likely push the other person away, and is unlikely to end well.

In this section of the book, you will learn how to do the prework prior to making an important ask so you can become even more influential, especially with your leadership. This prework is the runway that is a launch pad for influence. You'll do this by first learning how to have an ECO Mindset™, which is an acronym for Empathy, Curiosity, and Optimism. This is the world-class mental preparation that creates strategic empathy and fosters understanding, caring, and kinship with the other person. It also puts you in the right mental state to have a potentially emotionally charged or high- stakes conversation because it takes you out of your head and into the other person's. Next, you'll learn the tactical steps to structure your ask so you almost never get a no by using the Voice Amplifier Model™ and the Challenge Builder Template™. You will also learn how to amplify your voice and the feelings you create in yourself and others so you can make an even greater impression on your peers, subordinates, and leadership. The ripple effect of this is grand since amplifying your voice and the energy you transmute will be what spurs others to remember you and speak of you when you are not in the room.

C H A P T E R   1 1

ECO Mindset:
Developing Strategic Empathy

To become even more influential, especially under pressure or in high-stakes conversations, it's extremely helpful to develop strategic empathy toward the other person. Imagine standing in their shoes and then being explicit that you understand and care about their position before making your ask. Entering a conversation with clarity and optimism about how you'd like it to turn out for yourself and your counterpart will help defuse pushback before it happens. With an ECO Mindset you'll create the runway so your ask can take off and land successfully. In Sarah's case, it was landing on a salary package that was 7 percent or higher.

Adopting the empathy, curiosity, and optimism of the ECO Mindset is not necessarily for the other person. This process takes the focus off you and your ask so you can connect with the other person in a way that makes it more likely they'll listen to what you have to say. After this step, it's time to get tactical with how you structure your words or frame your ask.

Just like you would not put a roof on a home before the frame and walls are in place, there are a few other steps needed to prepare for a successful request. You will learn these additional steps in the sections to come, but first, let's look at the individual letters in ECO.

The E in ECO: Empathy

The E in ECO stands for empathy. Strategic empathy goes beyond mere understanding or shared feeling—it's about actively stepping into another's world and viewing it through their eyes. It requires a shift from our perspective to another's perspective. This shift doesn't entail losing sight of your objectives but means expanding your vision to include the goals, desires, and motivations of others.

When Sarah started shedding preconceived notions about her boss's intentions and instead focused on understanding the fears and challenges that drove his behavior, she was able to make progress toward her salary requirement. This did not mean condoning his prior actions but rather seeking to understand the why behind his original decision—why he seemed to have a short fuse, get agitated easily, and initially was not willing to budge. By not only

SHERYL KLINE, M.A. CHPC

standing in his shoes but taking on his persona to understand his perspective, Sarah gained insight into his behavior as well as felt compassion, which is important in the negotiation process.

According to an article in Psychology Today by renowned psychologist Rick Hanson, feeling cared for has been the primary driver of the development of the brain over the last 80 million years. Our ancestors— mammals, primates, hominids, and humans—survived, thrived, and passed on their genes by learning to find good mates, bond with their young, draw males in to provide for children, and create a community to help raise offspring.

In this context, being cared for was crucial to survival. Mammals that had no regard for being cared for did not pass on their genes. It's no wonder this feeling is the prerequisite to establishing trust and, therefore, influence.

Dr. Hanson shares that studies show that feeling cared about buffers against stress, increases positive emotions, promotes resilience and increases caring for others while also promoting good feelings in general. Over time, feeling cared for can gradually fill any holes in your heart left over from a time in which feeling cared for was not present or not present

228

enough.

When we take on someone else's persona, it's more than just being empathetic and considering what it must be like to be the other person. True strategic empathy and taking on another's persona is becoming the other person, standing in their shoes, looking at a situation from their vantage point, and feeling what they are feeling.

This is especially important, however challenging, to do for someone whom you do not see eye to eye with or someone who has wronged you in the past. But eliminating the process of establishing trust, caring, and safety prior to an ask is akin to baking bread before it's been allowed to rise. There's a high risk of falling flat or getting thrown out altogether.

While understandable, harboring negative feelings toward someone who has been challenging to deal with in the past will likely place us well behind the starting line when trying to gain buy-in. Developing strategic empathy is the prework that creates an environment for the other person to be more open to and intrigued by what you have to say. By taking the time to prepare our mindset, prime how our words are communicated and received, and connect with our counterparts in a way that is meaningful to them, we remove their hands from their ears, so they are better able to lean into what we have to say.

The C in ECO: Curiosity

Sounding truly curious requires us to be truly curious. The best way to communicate this effectively is to listen for the sake of listening and not listen to respond. Only about 10 percent of us listen effectively. According to the research in Psychology Today, we are often so distracted by technology and what is circling in our own mind, that we tend to listen to respond and not to actually hear or understand the other person.

No matter how good we think we are at listening while focused on something else, it typically does not go unnoticed. This can be detrimental to our personal and professional relationships.

For example, I used to hear the clickety-clack of the computer keyboard when talking to my husband about why he was at work. The message it sent was, "I don't care what you have to say." If we are not listening to listen, we are also missing valuable information that could help us when trying to gain buy-in down the road. Listening to listen does not just mean being quiet when someone else is speaking. It involves paying attention not only to words but to tone, cadence, and inflections that often accompany informative body language as well.

The words people say are, figuratively, just the tip of the iceberg. The research tells us that a mere 10 percent of an actual iceberg is above water, and 90 percent is below the surface. (OSU.edu, 2024). As we've discussed earlier, the words we speak make up a small percentage of what others perceive. What if we are on the receiving end? If we are actively listening and focus only on what we hear, that's roughly 10 percent of what we could be gaining from the other person. It's certainly better than attempting to listen while multitasking, but why not take in 90 percent more information that we can later use when building a case to gain buy-in?

A crucial aspect of influence is listening to absorb as much information as you can. One way to do this is to summarize or paraphrase what the other person is saying in your mind and explicitly out loud. When you do this, even if you are not spot-on, it will be extremely valuable for two reasons. First, your counterpart will likely correct you if you heard wrong, giving you even more information about what's important to them. Second, you will have demonstrated understanding and caring. Eye contact, nodding, and making sure that you wait until the other person is done speaking are also ways to listen effectively.

For Sarah, reframing her perspective meant getting curious. She started asking herself more questions, noting when she could answer them or when she needed to go directly to the source for an answer. What other pressures is my boss facing? What would make his job easier? What is most important to him? What consequences are lingering in the balance if expectations are not met? Who on the executive team is putting the pressure on him?

By asking these questions, Sarah wasn't just gathering information; she was demonstrating a deeper level of caring and connection as well as equipping herself with valuable information that she will be able to use when guiding her boss toward what she is asking for. Sarah was showing her boss that she valued and cared about his perspective as well as being invested in finding solutions that benefited them both.

For example, in an initial pre-influence conversation, Sarah expressed curiosity to her boss and learned a couple of pieces of new and important information. Unbeknownst to her, the company was in the very early stages of being positioned to be sold.

According to her boss, this placed a new layer of complexity and urgency on his objectives. She also learned the consequences of not hitting his objectives would be grave for her boss, for his entire team, and for the company. It was not only the executive team in her boss' ear. There were two key board members who were exerting their power and influence on him and his boss. Apparently, one of the board members had stepped in as Chief Operating Officer to steer the ship, and the company climate now felt a bit hostile.

Sarah's curiosity opened the door to creative problem-solving. It invited a collaborative approach where solutions could be cocreated rather than imposed. When Sarah became genuinely curious, she not only found ways to ease the pressures on her boss and make him feel safe about making a favorable decision about her raise, but she also positioned her ideas in a way that addressed his concerns and vision for what he wanted. Sarah did this by first taking on her boss's persona and asking herself, "What is most important to me? What pressure am I under? What would make my life easier? Where do I need the most help?"

Sarah determined the revenue goals the company needed to achieve, the optimal headcount, and the tactical strategy and accountability required for consistent progress. The value of having this airtight plan in place was priceless as the consequences of falling short in the coming months meant the value of the company might plummet, not to mention everyone's equity evaporating. Taking the time to gather this information, previously below the surface, accomplished two important things. First, it made Sarah's boss human, not just someone who consistently said no with seemingly little regard for what she had to say or what she was asking. Sarah moved from a place of judgment to a place of collaboration to solve a joint problem where her ask would become part of the solution rather than a request that could potentially make a situation worse. For example, let's say that Sarah was also asking for an extra headcount when budgets were frozen for hiring anyone new. A request for an additional headcount meant money exiting the company at a highly sensitive time.

Now that Sarah understood the complexity of her ask as well as what was on the line for her boss, she could position her ask in a way that would become the solution, a necessary piece of the revenue puzzle, for the extra revenue that needed to be generated. She reframed her ask from a give to a get. "Will you give me another headcount so I can hit my numbers?" became "We will get a 15 percent increase in revenue if we are able to fully execute our plan with the right team in place." Emphasize the pronouns we and us rather than I and me. Those who we trust and who care about us the most are like kin.

Creating kinship by using these inclusive pronouns rather than singular pronouns can help others feel like we share a similar goal.

The O in ECO: Optimism

The research tells us that we are biologically wired for negativity. (Gastelum 2021). The reason is, from an evolutionary standpoint, being on high alert keeps us safe and helps us avoid possible negative outcomes where we might perish. "The mind is like Velcro for negative experiences and Teflon for the positive ones," says neuropsychologist Rick Hanson.

Like the hardwired fight-or-flight response that helps us flee from something that threatens our life, like that sabertoothed tiger lurking around the corner, these evolutionary protection mechanisms are sometimes outdated and triggered in error. Not hitting our numbers at work or receiving a poor performance review might not be ideal, but we won't die. Being strategic and prepared to respond to ideal and not-so- ideal outcomes can be equally important, but catastrophizing and predicting an outcome that has not transpired yet is not helpful. It can send us flying around the Emotional Wheel™ like a clock that has gone mad. The ideal zone becomes a blur as our emotions whiz out of the green, past the yellow, and deep into the red.

The O in ECO stands for Optimism Starting from a place of optimism helps prime our brain for what we want and how we would like to feel rather than sending it down an imaginary road of doom that can spike our emotions and derail our ability to put our best foot forward. Starting from a place of optimism gives us a vision of where to begin reverse engineering, how we'll make our desired outcome happen, and how we'll diminish negative visualizations of something that has not happened yet.

This is not about being a Pollyanna or someone who sees everything through rose-colored glasses. Optimism in the face of adversity is a choice and a stance. It's a decision to focus on potential positive outcomes rather than dwell on the negative. For Julie, the sales director, adopting an optimistic mindset meant believing that every interaction with her colleague had the potential to be productive and that progress was always possible. With this perspective, she could reverse engineer how to make her desired outcome most likely to happen. Julie thought about what research she would need to do, how much she would need to prepare, and how she and her boss would feel once they agreed.

According to the research, optimism can also be contagious (Kliner & Lemon 2021). Mirror neurons, for example, are a class of nerve cells that exert their activity for both a specific motor act and when they observe the same or similar act performed by another individual. When Julie approached conversations with a positive outlook, her tone, and demeanor communicated that a positive outcome was possible. This shift in her approach was palpable, influencing not only her difficult colleagues' responses but also shifting the overall mood of the conversation from adversarial to collaborative.

It is also important to consider that how we feel, whether it's positive or negative, is a transfer of energy. According to Dr. Stephen Sideroff, electromagnetic signals from your body are picked up by others in your company. That could be why people who are negative or "needy" seem to drain our energy, while those who are positive can lift us up when we are down. When we are looking to enter a high-stakes negotiation or take a stance where we want to be highly influential, what we think, how we portray ourselves, and the energy we emit can all have an impact on the outcome we are trying to achieve.

The ECO Mindset Model™ assists you in preparing

your mindset prior to any crucial conversation or high-stakes moment where you are looking to influence an individual or a group. It is a tool to help you get out of your head and into that of your counterpart(s) and then reverse engineer the outcome you are looking for. Here are a few questions to ask yourself to help you develop an ECO Mindset prior to your next high-stakes conversation or presentation.

Empathy: Have I considered what it is like to stand in my counterpart's shoes?

Curiosity: Do I know what's important to the other person, what they are afraid of or concerned about, what pressure they are under, what is causing them stress, what they need, or what would make their life easier/better?

Optimism: How do I want this situation to turn out? What's a win-win for everyone involved?

Here's an amazing example of a female executive who was and continues to be highly influential:

Lani Phillips is a renowned and highly recognized technology and diversity, equity, and inclusion (DEI) industry leader, a former Microsoft Channel Sales executive who drove over $53 billion in revenue through a partnership ecosystem, and a Microsoft Circle of Excellence Awards winner. She has received numerous other industry awards, including CRN's Inclusive Channel Leaders and Most Powerful Women of the Channel: Power 100 awards, Insights Success's Top 10 Most Influential Women in the Cloud award, and the Linkage Women in Leadership Executive Impact Award.

Lani built an ECO Mindset before she was even familiar with what the acronym meant. From an early age, Lani was taught to be a leader and not a follower, to think for herself, to go against the grain, and to speak up for herself. This required a high level of influence that was not always easy to come by, and it required a high level of empathy for herself when things did not go her way. She also had to be curious about how resilient she'd need to be to bounce back and keep making progress.

There was one instance early on in her career when Lani and her team did not hit their sales target. According to Lani, this was a big miss at the time. She counts this experience as one of her few regrets, though it's not a regret because her team missed their sales target. In fact, Lani owned her mistakes and learned what to do differently so that the following year, she and her team blew the doors off their sales targets. Lani regrets this experience because she did not speak up for herself when someone in leadership shamed her in front of her boss and her peers at the sales meeting when her team fell short.

Lani did speak up to her boss and even her boss's boss, but she never said anything directly to the person who shamed her. Lani now reflects on the experience, saying, "If you wait and let other people tell your story, they're going to tell whatever narrative they want. And that's [when] I learned other people will take credit for your story or not tell your story accurately." In other words, tell your own story, always.

Sometimes, building an ECO Mindset (developing empathy, curiosity, and optimism) starts with us before we can use it to prepare to influence others. Lani learned early on to be empathetic toward herself. After receiving counseling when her mother passed away from cancer when she was just 12 years old, a therapist told her that she would have to learn how to mother herself. That resulted in Lani's ability early on to have empathy for herself, curiosity around the support she needed to move forward, and an innate ability to remain optimistic, even in the most difficult of moments. Applying an

ECO Mindset to herself, and later to high-stakes conversations with colleagues and clients, helped Lani drive billions in revenue, gain the respect of her leadership, and be widely recognized as a change agent in her industry. It also gave her the strength to take action on her next important move as a powerful leader, becoming the founder and CEO of FullCircle Leadership Group.

Whether you are at a point in your career where you are the most influential person in the room or still need buy-in from your leadership or board, the ECO Mindset model is the launchpad to becoming highly influential and spurring yourself or others into taking action.

Building Trust Through the ECO Mindset

Trust is the bedrock of influence. When Sarah adopted the ECO Mindset, she started to build trust with her boss, who felt that she understood his point of view even if they did not initially see eye to eye. Just like influence may not happen in one interaction, the trust between Sarah and her boss did not materialize overnight; it was the result of consistent, empathetic, curious, and optimistic interactions. Each conversation that ended positively added another brick to Sarah's position of influence.

ECO Mindset in Practice: Real-Life Applications

Sarah's success with the ECO Mindset wasn't limited to her boss. She found that these principles had broader applications. From leadership to client interactions and from team collaboration to personal relationships, having an ECO Mindset became her North Star.

In leadership, an ECO Mindset encourages a leader to be empathetic to team members' needs, curious about their ideas and feedback, and optimistic about their potential and the team's direction. This mindset fosters an environment where team members feel seen, heard, and motivated.

In client interactions, an ECO Mindset helps in understanding clients' underlying needs, asking the right questions to unearth deeper insights, and maintaining a positive outlook on the client relationship, even when facing challenges.

In team collaboration, an ECO Mindset promotes a culture of mutual respect, open- mindedness, and a shared vision for success. It encourages team members to look beyond their individual tasks and see the value in each other's contributions.

In personal relationships, the ECO Mindset strengthens bonds by fostering deeper connections, encouraging genuine interest in each other's lives, and setting the stage for you to make an ask or deliver some tough love. The message that is communicated to the other person with the ECO Mindset Model is: You are heard understood, and I care about you.

Expanding the ECO Mindset Beyond Individual Interactions

While the ECO Mindset Model might begin with a one-on-one interaction with a boss, the principles can be expanded to teams, departments, and entire organizations. A collective ECO Mindset can transform organizational culture, leading to a more engaged workforce, innovative problem-solving, and a positive work environment. Imagine if part of the preparation for an upcoming meeting was for all attendees to use the ECO Mindset Model to prepare, looking at problems through their colleagues' perspectives. How would it impact the collaboration, productivity, and final outcome?

Sustaining the ECO Mindset

Preparing to be highly influential during a crucial conversation, presentation, or any other high- takes moment is a great start, but it's important to be consistent and to make a conscious decision each day to lead with empathy, curiosity, and optimism—even when past experiences may encourage a more guarded or skeptical stance. For Sarah, and indeed for any professional, sustaining an ECO Mindset required practice and reinforcement. It involved reflecting on interactions, seeking feedback, and willingness to adjust approaches based on outcomes.

Challenges and Misconceptions About the ECO Mindset Model

Implementing the ECO Mindset is not without its challenges. It can be difficult to remain empathetic toward someone who is persistently difficult or to stay curious in the face of routine. Optimism can also be hard to sustain in an environment where you have experienced past failures. Like anything else, developing an ECO Mindset will take practice to develop consistency. Try practicing during low-stakes interactions—typically, family members or friends are great for this. You do not have to be heading into conflict to use an ECO Mindset. Let's say you are going to have lunch with a friend. Before you meet up and share how you've been, take a minute to stand in his or her shoes. Think as if you were them, experiencing what they've been experiencing or in the situation they are in.

There are also common misconceptions about the ECO Mindset Model. Empathy, for example, is not about being soft or yielding; it's about understanding. Curiosity is not about prying or being nosy; it's about genuine engagement and caring. Even if you do not care about the other person, do your best to develop curiosity so you can demonstrate caring. Curiosity is a leadership superpower. It is one of the most important connection- and trust-building tools you can have. (Mether, 2023).

Empathy, Curiosity, and Optimism are not just words; they are powerful tools that, when combined, can change the entire landscape of communication and influence while taking the focus and pressure off you. Let's look at a couple of real-life examples to help give the ECO Mindset Model some further context so you can think about how to apply it to situations that are important to you.

Case Study: Technology Sector—Vanessa's Visionary Leadership

Vanessa, a tech company CEO, recognized the importance of fostering a culture of innovation and collaboration. However, she noticed that her male- dominated executive team was sometimes dismissive of female colleagues' ideas. Vanessa implemented the ECO Mindset to transform the dynamic.

Strategic Empathy: Vanessa held individual meetings

245

to understand each executive's perspective and challenges, ensuring that each felt heard and valued.

Curiosity: She encouraged open brainstorming sessions, asking probing questions that allowed everyone to contribute meaningfully.

Optimism: Vanessa led by example, maintaining a positive outlook on the potential of diverse teams to drive innovation. Her optimism was infectious, leading to a more inclusive atmosphere and a spike in creative solutions from a now-energized team.

Case Study: Healthcare—Tracy's Collaborative Healing

Tracy, a hospital administrator, was tasked with improving interdisciplinary collaboration between departments, which was essential for patient care but hindered by departmental silos.

Strategic Empathy: She initiated shadowing programs where staff from different departments would spend a day in another department, experiencing their colleagues' roles firsthand.

Curiosity: Tracy hosted roundtable discussions, prompting staff from various specialties to share insights into their processes and challenges.

Optimism: She celebrated small victories in improved

246

patient outcomes due to better collaboration, reinforcing the belief that together, they could overcome the challenges of a fragmented system.

In these two scenarios, the female leaders used the ECO Mindset Model in preparation for their influence. They built the runway for their ability to be highly influential.

C H A P T E R   1 2

Amplify Your Voice

If developing an ECO Mindset is the runway, learning how to amplify your voice is rocket fuel. How you structure your conversations will help articulate your perspective in a way that you almost never get a firm no.

The essence of amplifying your voice in any setting, particularly in the workplace, is about ensuring your voice is heard and valued by those around you, especially your boss or those who can help champion your efforts. A recent client, Beth, who is a cyber security marketing manager, had a challenge to amplify her voice for a DEI initiative within her company. The initiative did not have much of a budget or total buy-in from her leadership on how important DEI was for the employees and for the company's bottom line. She felt like her boss was lending the minimum support because she had to and not because she believed in the importance of the DEI initiative. When requesting funding for any DEI project, the answer was usually, "No, we don't have the budget."

Beth's journey to turning her boss into a champion for her efforts rather than a roadblock was not met without opposition. What helped her breakthrough was her ability to properly prepare her ECO Mindset and to Amplify what she had to say when opening the conversation with her boss. This helped her become a leader who gains buy-in for an initiative that will benefit her colleagues and the company, even long after she is gone.

Let's look at how Beth turned a cursory nod of approval into enthusiastic backing and brought her boss on as an ally who championed her efforts.

How to Amplify Your Voice Step #1: Caring for Your Counterpart

For Beth to transform her boss from a passive endorser to an active champion for her DEI initiative, she knew she had to use a different approach to communicate her message and the value of it. Beth went from asking permission for funding to carefully and strategically building a plan to Amplify her voice so it would be heard, valued, and respected. Let's look at how she created an opportunity to have a second chance or to continue the conversation without being stopped in her tracks.

If developing an ECO Mindset™ is the mental preparation for our runway to be highly influential, developing a caring and confident mindset is the wind beneath our wings. Tone, gestures, and cadence can make the other person feel cared for and safe and, therefore, more ready for what we have to say. This is especially true in situations that have been contentious or lacked forward progress. For example, what we are thinking can impact our actions and determine if we sound condescending, caring, confident, or fearful. This can be communicated via arm gestures, which can signal confidence (arms open) or fear (arms crossed), or via tone, which can sound angry (loud) or timid (soft and ending sentences with a rising inflection). Mental preparation in the ECO Mindset Model™ is the prework we do to peel our counterpart's hands off their ears so they are more likely to lean in and listen when we amplify what we have to say.

For Beth, the first step was ensuring her boss that she was heard and understood, even if they did not see eye to eye on everything. During their second meeting, when Beth acknowledged and validated her boss, it wasn't about flattery; it was about genuinely understanding and expressing that understanding of her perspective, priorities, and the pressures she faced. By acknowledging the economic climate and the company's focus on cost-cutting and revenue generation, Beth created a common ground—a shared reality from which to build her case.

Because Beth had invested time in being curious about the nuances of her boss's challenges, what was important to her, and the company's strategic direction before their second meeting, Beth was able to frame the DEI initiative not just as a moral imperative but as a strategic one aligned with the company's goals. The first time Beth approached her boss for funding, it sounded something like, "We'd like to bring in speakers, create a mentorship program, and support our employees in feeling seen, included, and as valuable contributors. To get started, we will need $20,000 a year."

The second time she approached her boss; Beth did not talk about herself or make an ask initially. Instead, she took time to explicitly acknowledge and validate her boss first. She said, "It seems like our budget is extremely tight this quarter, and I completely understand."

Reflection:

What is a past conversation that you can go back to, or a future conversation to prepare for, which you can acknowledge and validate the other person's perspective by saying, "It seems/sounds/feels like _?

_____

_____

_____

Amplify Your Voice Step #2: Facts as Foundation

When Beth first approached her boss, the DEI initiative didn't have a clear benefit to her boss or to the organization. This was a new initiative with no proven track record or proof of return on investment. While Beth felt strongly that it was the right thing to do, that was not enough to get funding in the current economic climate. Beth's next move was to create a wall of indisputable facts that would be difficult for her boss to knock over. Before their second meeting, she meticulously gathered data and research showing the tangible benefits of a diverse workforce on innovation and profitability. This wasn't just about presenting data; it was about translating data into a compelling narrative that supported the DEI initiative's value proposition. Beth knew that growth was a focus for the remainder of the year and that numbers must be hit.

Reflection:

What is a fact about an ask you would like to make that be transformed into a compelling narrative?

_____

_____

_____

Amplify Your Voice Step #3: Sharing Your Point of View:

We must present our ideas clearly if we want others to understand us clearly. The first time around, Beth asked for "a budget" for her DEI initiative. She was stumbling a bit over her words, using too many words for what she had to say, and she was not clear on exactly what she was asking for. What did "a budget" mean? What was it for? What was the projected ROI?

As one of my business mentors, Donald Miller, says, "If you confuse, you'll lose." Keep this in mind whether you want a budget for a DEI initiative, a raise, another headcount, money to bring in a coach to help empower your team, or just about anything else where you require another person to get on board. Eventually, I helped Beth come up with a clear and defined ask: $20,000 per year to cover two speakers, quarterly hybrid meetings, and a virtual awards ceremony at the end of the year to recognize outstanding achievements. Based on the research on the desire for community, belonging, and support, the projected ROI was $200,000 to be recovered in employee retention, productivity, and company profitability.

Here are a couple of important ways for you to formulate a clear and powerful ask:

1. Be specific but give a range.

    According to research at the Columbia Business School, offering a range rather than a fixed amount comes across as more flexible and polite. This can also trigger what the legendary social psychologist Robert Cialdini calls reciprocity, leading to more favorable counter offers and potentially better deals. Just make sure you'll be happy with the lower range.

According to social psychologist David Loschelder, for example, using unconventional numbers, like odd numbers, can increase your earning potential during salary negotiations. Asking for a raise of $12,000 or $17,000 per year is better than asking for $10,000 to $15,000. Even better is asking for $12,500 to 17,500 because it will feel well thought out. Loschelder does warn, however, not to get too specific, down to the penny, or we may not be taken seriously. (Papadopoulos, 2023).

2. Get your head in the game.

Often if we are not clear or if we feel unworthy, we tend not to be explicit about our ask, and we might use too many words that are distracting and not relevant. The reason why "we confuse, we lose" is true in practice is because our brains seek answers and make sense of what's being asked of us. If we are searching and sorting through too many bits of information, we get overwhelmed with information, and there is no clear path to yes.

If we are vague and sound uncertain of our ask, it is more work for the other person to figure out what we are saying. It's almost always easier to say no to a question when we feel confused or unclear. (Stanley, 2017).

Imagine that you are not feeling well and go to the doctor. In response to your ailment, your doctor says, "We'd like to remove an organ, but we are uncertain of which one." Would your mind start going a mile a minute? I know mine would. Which organ? Why? What did you find that made you decide? Is my life in danger? How do you figure out which organ? How much will it cost? How much work will I miss?

Instead, what if your doctor said, "We need to remove your tonsils and adenoids. This procedure is not serious at all, and it will not have any serious side effects or significant recovery time. You can expect to miss one day of work." Now you are clear on exactly what is happening and don't have to fill in the gaps or create stories that are not based on truth.

Reflection:

What is a specific monetary ask that you have coming up, and what will your range be? This can be in your professional or personal life.

Amplifying Nonpecuniary Asks

When we share our points of view and amplify our voices, the outcomes are not always related to money or monetary gains. For example, in a leadership meeting where building visibility is important, we might appreciate not being spoken over by a certain peer, or perhaps we would like to be put on more challenging projects. Amplifying our voice means being explicit as it relates to money or other things that are valuable to us. We may even find that our peer was unaware of cutting us off or that our boss had no idea we were interested in different projects. After a meeting where you are being spoken over by a peer, for example, ask for a private conversation with your colleague so you can come up with a solution. Your ask may sound something like, "It seems like you're knowledgeable and excited about this project, which is fantastic (acknowledge and validate). However, during our all-hands meeting, when it was time for me to present, you interrupted me." Notice that you're not expressing an opinion or judgment here, just a fact. This is a great time for a pause to listen to what your colleague has to say.

Again, to be explicit means to know the desired response you are looking for. Do you want an apology? Do you want to collaborate on a solution, so it does not happen again? Do you have a suggestion for a solution? When we are building influence for an ask that does not involve money, it may be helpful to have one or two solutions in mind. In regard to being spoken over, perhaps the solution could be for your colleague to go first when presenting or to accept a reminder from you if it happens again.

Reflection:

Do you have a nonpecuniary (not related to money) ask? Perhaps you are building a case to attend a conference or a leadership meeting that is a level-up. Or you wish to influence your partner on a vacation destination.

_____

_____

_____

Amplify your voice. Step #4: Practice

World-class performers, whether Olympians, rock stars, classical musicians, speakers, or CEOs, do not wing it or debut on the main stage without practicing at smaller venues first. Whether you are a manager looking to ascend to vice president or a parent who wants to have more influence on her teenager, crucial conversations with potentially a lot on the line need to be practiced in low-stakes environments prior to the main event. You could ask a colleague whom you trust or a family member to role-play with you or simply look in the mirror. As we discussed in the Confidence section, competence builds confidence, and this is one step you have control over that differentiates world-class performers who are well rehearsed from amateurs who haven't properly prepared. You might be wondering how much you need to practice or how you'll know when you're prepared. As a general rule, the more there is riding on the conversation or presentation and the more nervous you are, the more practice and preparation are needed. Remember to decide on the outcome you would like to have, think through your gaps or where you'd like to improve, and then commit to specific days and times to practice and report to an accountability partner.

Beth placed a very high level of importance on her meeting with her boss. She blocked out 30 minutes each morning to practice for the two weeks leading up to her meeting. To determine if she was truly prepared, I role-played the meeting with her. With me in the role of her boss, we went through each possible scenario, and I did my best to ask uncomfortable questions and be uncertain at first so she would feel familiar and comfortable responding. We also role-played favorable outcomes so she could practice responding to those. A tool for you to tie everything together is the Voice Amplifier Model™:

1. Acknowledge/Validate: Let the other person know that you hear them and understand what they are saying. For example, "It seems like staying within our budget and driving sales is top priority, and I understand completely." Remember that validating is not the same as agreeing. You're simply making someone feel seen and heard.

How can you acknowledge and validate another's perspective?

_____

_____

_____

2. Facts: Do your homework to uncover data, research, or proof that backs up your ask.

What facts can you uncover that are indisputable? Do you have to back up your ask?

_____

_____

_____

3. Point of View: Be able to articulate what your ask is or what you are trying to convey.

Can you clearly state what an ideal outcome would be?

_____

_____

_____

4. Practice: What is most important to practice so that you are as prepared as possible to make you ask? A hint: Practicing your ask, your tone, cadence, and how you articulate what you want is just as important as the rest of the conversation.

What is most important for you to practice, and when will you do it?

_____

_____

Amplifying Your Voice is Building a Coalition for Change

Amplifying our voice does not rest on your shoulders alone; it requires a coalition of champions. For example, Beth knew that to truly institutionalize the DEI initiative, she needed allies among leaders who were in power. She began identifying potential champions across the organization, using her newfound influence strategies to create a network of advocates. She did this by connecting with key stakeholders based on what was important to them. By presenting her ideas in a way that resonated with various stakeholders, she began building a movement within the company. This was because what Beth was asking became a solution to her peers' and leadership's concerns rather than simply an ask for something she wanted.

For example, Beth's boss was a veteran, a woman, and a woman of color. Her boss also had three daughters. Rather than leading her conversation with how Beth felt DEI was important, she honored the accomplishments that her boss had made and learned more about the work environment her boss liked to create for her daughters. Beth was also very explicit about the research she'd done on the dollar value and increased innovation of a diverse team, specifically that cash flow increased two and a half times per employee with a diverse workforce (Reiners & Urwin, 2024). and companies were 70 percent likelier to capture a new market share (Hewlett, Marshall, Sherbin, 2013). Now she was speaking her boss's language! Building this coalition with her boss would amplify Beth's impact significantly more than if she kept her DEI ideas and ambitions to herself.

The Ripple Effect When We Amplify Our Voice

Beth's story of amplifying her influence around her DEI initiative serves as a case study of how one voice when strategically and passionately raised, can create a ripple effect of positive change. From securing the support of her boss to engaging an entire organization, Beth's approach exemplified the principles of influence, strategic communication, and the transformative power of explicitly recognizing her boss's concerns before her own.

It's clear that our ability to amplify our voice is both an art and a science. It's an art in the way it requires creativity and adaptability and science in its need for strategy and evidence. By mastering this balance, professionals like Beth—and you—

can amplify their causes, champion their initiatives, and, ultimately, leave a lasting impact on their organizations and communities.

Case Study: Finance Sector—Amplifying Impact with Emma

Emma, a seasoned executive at a leading investment firm, faced a significant hurdle: She wanted to influence the board to adopt a new sustainable investment strategy. Despite its potential for long-term growth and environmental impact, the board was hesitant due to unfamiliarity with the approach and perceived short-term risks.

Emma decided to amplify her influence. She started by ensuring she understood the board members' concerns, demonstrating empathy, and acknowledging the risks they perceived. Then, she presented indisputable data showing the success of sustainable investments in other firms and the growing trend of adopting environmental, social, and governance (ESG) criteria among investors. By connecting the firm's mission with the global shift toward sustainability, Emma aligned her proposal with the company's values and future growth objectives. Her well-prepared presentation, backed by solid data and a clear vision, won over the board and produced results that even surprised Emma. Her initiative led to the successful implementation of a sustainable investment strategy that won the firm three of its largest clients within six months after the strategy shift was in place. It also improved the firm's market standing by 15 percent. Emma was proud that she had the courage to push her strategy through as well as of the ripple effects it would have for years to come.

Case Study: Education — Amplifying Voices with Dr. Nina

Dr. Nina, a university dean, recognized the need to amplify the representation of women in STEM fields within her institution. She was determined to secure more funding and resources for women-focused STEM programs but knew that she had to approach the predominantly male board of trustees strategically. She built her case by first engaging in one-on-one conversations with each trustee, listening to their priorities, and acknowledging the constraints of the university's budget. In her proposal, Dr. Nina cited research on the benefits of diversity in educational outcomes and innovation, as well as success stories from other institutions.

By tying the initiative to the university's core values of excellence and innovation and demonstrating how the programs could position the university as a leader in STEM education, Dr. Nina was able to secure unanimous board approval. Her efforts led to a significant increase in female enrollment in STEM programs and set a precedent for gender inclusivity across the campus.

Case Study: FinTech Innovations — Lara's Leadership Leap

Lara, a chief technology officer at a FinTech company, was passionate about implementing a new blockchain-based transaction system that promised to revolutionize the industry. However, she needed to influence her conservative CEO, who was wary of the volatility associated with cryptocurrencies.

Lara listened intently to her CEO's concerns about security and regulatory issues, validating his points before presenting her counterarguments. She aligned her innovative solution with the company's goal of staying at the forefront of financial technology, emphasizing enhanced security features and efficiency gains. Maintaining an unwavering belief in the technology, Lara painted a vivid picture of the company setting industry standards with its pioneering system, leading to the eventual buy-in and approval from her CEO.

Lara's initiative was not pushed through in one meeting; instead, she amplified her voice by consistently connecting with her CEO on what was important to him, persisting when she hit a roadblock or faced pushback, and being crystal clear on what she was asking. Because she amplified her voice with her CEO, Lara's ability to have an even greater impact was magnified.

These case studies exemplify how female leaders in various sectors have successfully used influence to change mindsets, drive innovation, and lead their companies toward a more productive, profitable, and just future.

Reflection:

What is an initiative, big or small, for which you are trying to gain buy-in, and how can you amplify your voice to make it happen? (It may be helpful to have a look at the Voice Amplifier Model™. Also, who or what else will this impact if you get a yes?

_____

_____

_____

While we are in daily conversations where we attempt to influence and amplify our voices, influencing our leaders can be both challenging and rewarding for us and for our organization. But how do we influence, lead our leaders, and remain respectful while shifting sometimes cemented perspectives? The next part of the Fearless Female Leadership Influence section will show you how to do just that.

You will first learn the psychology behind why it's a good idea to initially seek a no rather than a yes, the importance of influencing ourselves prior to attempting to influence others, the impact of which pronouns we choose to use, and, finally, the three steps to follow to craft your communication so you can affirm what you have to say and make progress toward gaining buy-in from your leadership.

CHAPTER 13

Affirm Your Ask:
Challenging Others to See
Your Perspective and to Take Action

It is often uncomfortable to affirm what we want and gain buy-in, especially for women. Why? In addition to being labeled as "pushy" or "bitchy" when asking for what we want, women also have internalized messages that we should not promote ourselves and that our work will speak for itself (Linda Babcock and Sara Laschever research from their book *Women Don't Ask: Negotiation and Gender Divide*). Combine that with the cultural and social indoctrinations of not being raised to speak up, brag, or ask for what we want and deserve, and it's no wonder affirming a request is easier and more common for our male counterparts.

Unfortunately, it's a myth that our work speaks for itself, and it will only add to the gender divide if we do not increase our visibility by becoming even more vocal about our accomplishments, talents, and goals. The more comfortable we get with this, the more comfortable we will be asking for what we want, therefore having greater visibility and impact. In this chapter, we'll gain an even better understanding of why we clam up when our gut and our hearts tell us to speak up. Why getting to a no is more important than getting to a yes when making an ask. Why and how we sometimes get in our own way and, finally, why the pronouns we choose can make or break our attempt to gain buy-in. Then, we'll cover the three strategies to affirm what we are asking for with confidence, so we almost never get a no.

Human beings are biologically hardwired to seek comfort and safety (Blackmon 2013). That seems to make sense since most of us do not seek out uncomfortable situations to put ourselves in. In a work setting, many times, it is just easier not to speak up or go against the status quo. Whether trying to land a new role, receive the best compensation package, have a bigger voice in meetings, or set new boundaries that contribute to your current and long-term success, affirming an ask may require getting comfortable with the uncomfortable.

Speaking up and affirming what we believe in is what has shaped the freedom, comforts, and inventions we enjoy today. For example, one woman who paved the way for all of us was Bessie Coleman, the first American woman to earn an international pilot's license. Bessie earned her initial pilot's license in France and since she was unable to receive a commercial pilot's license due to gender and racial bias, she focused on stunt flying. On September 3, 1922, Bessie returned to her hometown of Waxahachie, Texas, where large crowds gathered to see the first public flight by an African American woman. Bessie refused to perform for segregated crowds and influenced the organizers to allow everyone to come into the viewing area through the same entrance. Eventually, she founded a school for black aviators. (History Extra 2018). Bessie Coleman spoke up and spoke out against segregation. She undoubtedly pushed others outside of their comfort zone when she made her request, and it would not be unreasonable to assume that making such an ask was uncomfortable for her as well.

Another trailblazer was Grace Hopper, a computer scientist, mathematician, and pioneer of computer programming. Her legacy lives on through the Grace Hopper Celebration, a national conference for technologists. Along with Grace, six of the first modern computer programmers were women: Frances Snyder Holberton, Jean Jennings Bartik, Kathleen McNulty Antonelli, Marlyn Wescoff Meltzer, Ruth Lichterman Teitelbaum, and Frances Bilas Spence. Known as the ENIAC Programmers, they were not recognized until they were well into their 70s.

Eventually, a programmer and Harvard undergrad named Kathy Kleiman learned about these women and how they helped create early computer programs to calculate artillery trajectories at speeds that were much faster than human calculations. Kathy shared their stories, inspiring a long-overdue period of awards and honors for the ENIAC Programmers. In 1997, all six women were inducted into the Women in Technology Hall of Fame (WITI 2024), and the U.S.

Army has supercomputers named Jean, Kay, and Betty to recognize three of the women who helped make the world's first computer a reality (Little 2021). These women did not have the opportunity to affirm their voices, but thankfully, Kathy Kleinman did it for them when she had the chance.

Whether you plan to go down in history or not, what is in your heart and gut is no less important. It is a gift that should be shared, and affirming your ask may require you to challenge your current circumstances and challenge those who are in power so they understand the value and impact of what you have to say.

Affirming Your Ask: The Paradox of Yes and No

The conventional wisdom for driving others toward yes is often less effective than one might think. "Yes" can sometimes feel like a trap to the receiver, a surrender of autonomy. Instead, when your counterpart is free to say no, it can be empowering, paradoxically leading a counterpart to our perspective while maintaining their sense of control.

"Yes" is a sneaky trickster that puts us on high alert, especially when we are trying to gain buy-in, certainly from someone who does not know us well, someone who is not on the same page, or someone who is controlling and does not want to be challenged. Have you ever had a call with a telemarketer that went something like this: "Hello. This is Bob from the Clean Water Alliance. Is it important to you to have clean water to drink?" It feels like a trick, right? The telemarketer is boxing us into a corner so they can ask for money. Even my gentle black Lab will come out fighting to defend herself when trapped in a corner. We do not want to set our counterparts up to feel threatened or feel like they must defend their own interest. When we immediately look for a yes, we trample over the other person's concerns, not demonstrating one of our most basic needs: feeling understood and cared for.

Saying no makes us feel in control (Martin 2024). If given the option to walk away rather than be trapped in a corner, my black Lab would either demonstrate "no" by walking away or choose to come over and say hello because she does not feel threatened.

If my friendly dog felt physically trapped, she may feel scared, not in control, and therefore get aggressive.

Assigning control to the other person can be important for our subordinates, clients, bosses, or anyone else we find ourselves negotiating with because it grants agency to the other person. The research tells us that we tend to better support what we have a hand in creating (Blomquist 2024). When feeling in control enough to say no and respond in a way that makes sense to use, we become a cocreator of a joint vision.

How you accomplish this is like a chess move that requires a strategic set up. In Part 1 of this chapter, we covered a proven process to build trust and create safety with your counterpart and to also transfer the focus from us to the other person. This laid the runway for others to listen to what we have to say. In Part 2, we began to structure our words by acknowledging and validating what is important to the other person first, anchoring our point of view in fact, and then sharing our point of view clearly and succinctly. Now, in Part 3, you are ready to lead your counterpart to take action toward what you are asking for. You're ready to affirm your ask. This is where it is important to get comfortable being uncomfortable. The reward being your counterpart will lean in and listen to what you have to say. We are going to put your counterpart in the driver's seat so they feel in control while being compelled to steer toward where you want them to go. This is because your ask will become a solution for them rather than a request for them to give something up. To create this sense of control for your counterpart, shift their mindset, and help open them to taking action on your behalf, it's important for you to get in the back seat.

Affirming Ourselves-Our Toughest Opponent

Cindy (not her real name) is a property manager for a large commercial real estate management company. It is the nature of her job to be highly connected to the work that she loves. Cindy can be contacted at any time of day or night most days of the week, and her role is extremely fast paced when she is not responding to urgent requests. The days are long, though, and the weekdays bleed into the weekends. Having the energy to be present with her children was increasingly more difficult. Her understanding husband missed seeing Cindy as much as he used to, and her interactions with friends were reduced to text messages or an occasional phone call in the car. Cindy had not seen her two best friends for over two years. On top of this, she started getting migraines, which she had never experienced before. This impacted her, her family, and her ability to be a sustainable high performer at work. Cindy came to the realization that she would not be able to keep up the pace her role demanded. She was torn, though, because she was otherwise very happy with her role, with her colleagues and boss, and with being the primary earner in her family.

Sometimes, the first person we need to influence and affirm is ourselves. If a situation is not working, we must ask ourselves what we need and affirm we are worthy of receiving it. In Cindy's case, she needed boundaries so she could sustain the impact she was having at work and at home. Before influencing those around her and affirming her ask for these boundaries, Cindy had to affirm the ask for herself, affirm that she was worthy, deserving, and safe to set the boundaries she thought were important to be able to sustain her work and her impact.

Sometimes it is also important to slow down, take a pause, and look back at what our highest sense of integrity is, what makes us feel congruent. Are we living our three words that we declared in the Clarity chapter to the best of our ability at work and at home? What is the legacy we want to leave behind, and how do we want to be remembered at work and by the people who matter most to us? It is important to think about the outcome or change we would like to make that will allow us to shift so we can have the impact we hold in our hearts. Finally, we can ask ourselves a question that can influence us to take action. Cindy's question was, "Based on my goal of continuing to be a top performing property manager, to have a loving marriage, to nurture my friendships, and to be a mother whom my kids will remember as present, caring, kind, and fun, is there something I need to start or stop doing immediately?" This opened Cindy's eyes to just how important affirming her ask to herself was.

Affirm Your Ask with the Proper Pronouns

When preparing for a crucial conversation, or any high-stakes interaction, we typically prepare by knowing what we are asking for, why our point of view is important, and why what we are presenting will be beneficial to the other person. If we say something like, "In order for me to hit my numbers, I need another headcount." It is important to understand that pronouns such as me, you, and I infer separation between you and your counterpart(s). We risk sending the message that we are opponents rather than teammates, which can put others, consciously or unconsciously, on high alert to protect their position. Shifting from me and I to "we" and "us" brings the other person onto our side and onto the same team. It closes the gap, so you do not lose them in the chasm between their wants and needs and yours. A shift in pronouns for the sentence above could look like: "In order for us to hit the numbers we are shooting for ..." Now your counterpart feels understood and like you are on their team. We have created what Daniel Pink calls "kinship," or closeness, in his book To Sell is Human. This level of trust is another runway that we can't afford not to build.

Affirming Your Ask Part 1: Connecting to Your Counterpart's Values

When Cindy first came to me for coaching, she was frustrated because of her boss's response to her asking for a more regular schedule and not being available on the weekends. Cindy got up the courage to meet with her boss, but she began the conversation with what she wanted and why. Upon receiving a no to both requests, Cindy felt like her boss did not care about her circumstances, and she was also questioning whether or not the career she chose was going to work with her growing family.

Rather than her frustration getting more intense or leading her to think about a new career, we had a conversation about how to affirm Cindy's ask by connecting with her boss first, prior to asking for a more predictable schedule or for the weekends off.

Framing an effective ask lies in aligning with your counterpart's values first. If Cindy, for example, understood this and took the time to connect her ask with her boss's integrity, she would have likely made more progress the first time she approached him. It's about drawing a clear, unambiguous line between what you're asking for and what the listener holds dear. This is different from acknowledging and validating what the other person wants to achieve, as we discussed in the Amplify chapter. It is more about the other person's integrity that is innate to them, such as being passionate about innovation, autonomy of employees, reputation in the industry, or support for emerging leaders.

Reflection:

For someone who you would like to influence, what is one aspect of their values that you could connect with when preparing to affirm your voice?

_____

_____

_____

Affirming Your Ask Part 2: Creating Common Ground and Building on Shared Objectives

Building on common goals fosters a sense of kinship and oneness, therefore building. Especially when we are attempting to have influence with our leadership, affirming our ask can be delicate because leaders are often asked to give up budget, time, or other resources. Asking to work towards a common goal or outcome will likely be a more welcome request than simply asking to hand something over. For example, if you'd like an additional headcount, think through what your boss needs as well. In Cindy's case, her boss wanted to sell to existing clients who had other buildings. This was important to Cindy, too, and she led with it, basing her ask on her ability to deliver with a more predictable schedule and fewer distractions from family events on the weekend.

Cindy's conversation with her boss began something like this: "We pride ourselves on building deep and unwavering relationships with our existing customers, so they will trust us with their other properties ..." When we speak to someone about something they care about deeply should this be 'care deeply about', we have their attention. When we don't, their attention is a fraction of the pie. Let's connect and capture our counterpart's attention by bringing them closer

with a common objective.

Reflection:

Now it's your turn! For an upcoming conversation or a conversation, you'd like to redo, what is one thing that is important to both of you?

_____

_____

_____

Affirm Your Voice Part 3: Creating a Challenge Questions

Like the rest of us, those with authority typically like to

feel powerful and safe. They likely do not want to make decisions that expose them or threaten their safety in any way. Protecting their safety can mean protecting their reputation, integrity, goals, competencies, and favorable perceptions of them from others. Often, leaders are asked questions that potentially threaten their safety, such as relinquishing more money for a raise, promotion, or headcount.

Can you assign your counterpart the feeling of control and transform your ask into a solution to a problem rather than a request? Those who master this way of framing questions can shift potentially confrontational standoffs to collaborative sessions where problem-solving is the focus and outcome. Getting a no is not simply an answer to a question. It can become a new and more effective pathway to move initiatives and ideas forward.

Let's have a look at how to use what we know is meaningful and important to the other person and frame a question where our ask is based on our counterpart's needs and not our own. What happens when we learn about the other person and communicate explicitly? More listening, more interest in what we have to say, and an increased likelihood of gaining buy-in (Shonk 2019).

The Challenge Builder Template: A Guide to Constructive Asks

The Challenge Builder Template is a step-by- step guide to constructing asks that pulls together what you've learned in this chapter so others are more likely to align with your perspective and ultimately with your ask. It's a process that can transform an absolute no into a maybe or a no for now, keeping the dialogue open and progressing. I developed the Challenge Builder Template as a step-by-step guide so you can have a coach of sorts to lead you through preparing for your next crucial conversation, presentation, or interview.

Questions from the Challenge Builder Template

What is important to the person/people you are trying to influence? (e.g., growth, autonomy of team, innovation, developing future leaders, etc.)

_____

_____

_____

What is a common goal or outcome for you and your counterpart? (e.g. ten percent growth)

_____

What is a question that includes what's important to the person/people and your common goal/outcome? Be sure to use the pronouns we and us rather than I and me. For example: "Our team's autonomy seems very important. Based on our goal of ten percent growth, would it be out of the question to add a headcount so we can get 10 times the return on investment and hit our sales goal?" Notice that this question is a no question as opposed to a yes question, making the other person feel in control.

What's your question?

Reflection:

What is a recent ask that you have made that you would adjust a bit based on what you've just learned? If you have an upcoming crucial conversation, what is an example of your challenge sentence using the Challenge Builder Template?

Affirming Your Ask Part 4: Practice and Role- playing for Success

Olympians do not begin their career competing at the Olympics. There are years, if not decades, of local, regional, national, and international competitions on the road to making this dream a reality. There are setbacks, failures, wanting to quit and give up, and then dusting off and continuing to move forward. The moments spent competing in the Olympics are a few pebbles of time compared to the vast mountain spent practicing when no one is looking or cheering them on.

Your Olympics, your vision for the leader you'd like to be, and the impact you'd like to have been is no less important. To have a bigger voice at the table, it will require practice—not simply showing up at the main event, asking for a promotion, salary package, raise, or to lead an initiative. as well as establishing yourself to be heard, valued, and respected even more.

You can get creative here with how you practice! Is

there a colleague whom you trust and who has your best interest at heart or a friend you can depend on? If not, use a mirror or any other imaginative way to get your "reps" in. Just like an Olympian, practice in low-stakes environments first before taking the main stage. This will help you to feel more competent, confident, and emotionally agile. If you are confident and able to regulate your emotions, your words will likely land on your counterpart that way, too. If we are confident in ourselves, it's easier for others to be confident in what we are asking for.

For example, Trish is a sales manager at a cybersecurity company. She found herself without a colleague with whom she felt comfortable practicing for her upcoming discussion with her boss about her wanting to be placed as a lead on an upcoming initiative. So, she turned to role-playing by herself. Recording ourselves can be an enlightening exercise; it allows for self-review and adjustment, honing both the content and delivery of the message. Trish's methodical rehearsal on her phone ensured she could evaluate her tone, pitch, and conviction behind her words until she achieved the confidence and clarity she sought. Trish committed to practicing until she rated herself an eight out of ten. After her first try, she thought she was a five.

With one week until the meeting, Trish committed to practicing for 15 minutes every weekday morning.

There is power in consistency and commitment. Trish's focus on improving and the process of doing her best helped her decline the temptation to worry about the outcome. She assumed her desired outcome would happen and reverse-engineered her most important practice tasks to make it happen.

The result? Trish felt deserving, qualified, and confident in her conversation with her boss. Her mental and tactical preparation resulted in Trish's boss agreeing to rethink how the team for the upcoming project would be structured and asked Trish to be prepared the following week to present her ideas to her boss's leadership team.

Trish's victory was not a definitive yes from her boss. Her victory was the courage to speak up and ask for what she wanted, commit to the process of making it happen, and make progress toward that goal.

In those 15 minutes before work for just five days, Trish was able to affirm her ask and was rewarded with newfound respect from her boss. She was also surprised with an invitation to present to the leadership team a level above her boss. Without practicing and being able to affirm her ask with confidence and conviction, she would have run the risk of sounding uncertain or unsure that she wanted, or was capable of doing, what she was asking for. Affirming our ask before others requires us to affirm our ask to ourselves first, and that takes practice—a practice that most are not willing to do or don't understand the importance of.

Practicing is rarely sexy or fun. There are no awards or recognition for practice, only the satisfaction of knowing you did your best to prepare and left no stone unturned.

After working with world-class athletes, Olympians, and some of the most influential female leaders in San Francisco, Silicon Valley, and across the country, I've found that the willingness to refine skills, hone what is already good, and do so when no one is looking or while in the solitude of a quiet gym, track, or office, before anyone else has arrived, is what sets the best apart from the rest.

Remember, proceed as if success is inevitable, and take control of how you prepare to affirm your ask. This level of preparation will ensure that when you are called, you are ready.

Reflection:

List an upcoming crucial conversation, when it is, and when you will practice. On a scale of 1 to 10, where are you currently, and where will you commit to being?

_____

_____

_____

When Affirming Your Ask Does Not Work

It's important to realize that gaining buy-in rarely happens in one conversation, and often, it takes more than one influential conversation. It's a campaign, a series of engagements, each building upon the last. It is vital to focus on incremental wins, how to move beyond the setbacks, and be ready to regroup and revisit the conversation as needed. Whether our no question leads to a yes or not, just the process of us planning out, articulating, and voicing our point of view in this new way likely means progress has been made.

Building influence, especially with our boss and often with our clients, is a long game. If we can greet initial resistance like a welcomed guest who offers useful information rather than an in-law who's making us crazy or an intruder who threatens our safety, we can keep moving in the right direction rather than two steps forward and four steps back. By mastering this shift in perspective and keeping our emotions in check, we catch the ball and keep running rather than getting sacked and pulled out of the game.

Sometimes, we make progress, and we do not even realize it! We can be so focused on getting the promotion, the additional headcount, buy-in on a new initiative, or even our vacation preference with our partners that we assume a no means never rather than no for now. Even when we meet resistance, there is value in our ask if we know how to move through it with optimism, gratitude, and an ability to see the gold that lies within the response that we did not want. One way to do this is to hold a high goodbye standard for yourself. In other words, when we have attempted to influence, and our counterpart is clearly not going to budge, rather than get upset or frustrated or keep asking only to risk making them upset, try this: "Bob, it seems like we are not seeing eye to eye, which is OK. I appreciate you spending the last 15 minutes with me to discuss bringing on an additional headcount. Would it be out of the question to reconnect on this next Tuesday?" Now, it's time to gather more data to support your ask.

When we affirm our ask, the golden rule is to affirm the ask no more than twice. First, acknowledge and validate the other's perspective, then mention an indisputable fact, and then share what your ask is by asking your "no" question. If you receive pushback the first time through, start again from the top by acknowledging and validating their perspective. If you are still not getting anywhere after the second time through, or if emotions from either of you are beginning to flare, it is typically clear that the conversation has moved along as far as possible. At this point, it is time to retreat, express gratitude, and re- prepare rather than risk emotions that could derail your progress. An example of what you could say is: "Bob, thank you so much for hearing me out. It seems like we are not seeing eye to eye, which is completely understandable. Let's circle back next week on Thursday or Friday. Which day/time is best for you?"

Tone Reminder

Remember the importance of tone. To express gratitude, it's important to feel grateful, not annoyed or frustrated. There is nothing more effective to derailing progress than allowing negative emotions via a negative tone into a conversation. In the face of pushback, stay in the "green" zone. Look at resistance as knowledge and as an affirmation that you are on the right track. Welcome it in, and feel grateful for the person, the progress, and the new knowledge you now have.

Case Study: Healthcare—Dr. Liu's Leadership in Medicine

Dr. Liu, a prominent figure in a large healthcare system, was passionate about integrating holistic health practices into conventional medical treatments. Despite her enthusiasm and expertise, she struggled to gain the support of her traditionally minded colleagues. Dr. Liu reflected on her commitment to patient-centered care and the potential of integrative medicine. She researched success stories, patient testimonials, and studies that highlighted the efficacy of her methods.

By consistently affirming the value of her work and its alignment with the healthcare system's mission, Dr. Liu eventually won the backing of her peers and the administration. Her program has since become a model for other healthcare institutions seeking to broaden their treatment paradigms.

C H A P T E R 1 4

Aspire:
Articulating Your Vision

"People will forget what you said, people will forget what you did, but people will never forget how you made them feel."

— *Maya Angelou*

Our aspiration for a better future, the flame that is in our gut and in our heart, is fanned not only by what we say but, even more importantly, by how we make others feel. It is the transfer of emotion that leaves a lasting impression on others and that ushers them, knowingly or unknowingly, to champion our efforts. Our level of effect helps us to join forces with those in power to turn our whisper into a roar so we can influence without abandon. When we attempt to influence others to champion our vision, it is not only important to know how to prepare our mindset and how to structure our communications. We must know how to communicate our commitment, care, and the emotion behind what we are asking for. The research tells us that emotion is a powerful driver behind decision-making (Lerner, Li, Valdesolo, Kassam, 2014). We can leave an important and lasting impression so others can see and feel why it's a good idea. If you aspire to influence others who can champion your efforts, you will first need to see and feel the outcome so they can, too. Our aspiration is a painting being explained to someone who cannot see, in a way that makes the image come to life and that makes their heart skip a beat with excitement and hope for a better future.

Our aspiration requires us to step into the position of a visionary, to dream and believe beyond our comfort zone, and to have faith in what's possible while not succumbing to what's likely. Once we grant ourselves permission to step outside the confines of the familiar, what we know to be certain, what others think we are capable of, or to step over the line into uncharted territory, we can transfer the energy of possibility from ourselves to a person or people who can help us. How we communicate our aspirations is the glue that holds together the trust, safety, and buy- in or progress that we have worked so hard to build.

Your Visionary Brain and How It Impacts Others

The human brain once thought to be more set or finite, is in a constant state of growth, change, and adaptation (Lafee, 2020). As we have different experiences, our thoughts and emotions can strengthen or weaken our memory depending largely on the level of emotion associated with the experience (Swaim, 2022). These experiences don't always have to be physical; they can be imaginary and still exhibit a similar response in the brain (Ali, 2022).

A study published in Neuron showed that imagining a threat, for example, generates almost the same response in the brain as experiencing it in real life. The same principle can be used for success. Visualizing the scenario of succeeding in a difficult situation or achieving your goals can activate the same areas in your brain as physically experiencing this scenario. This promotes the brain's ability to change in a positive way in a process called neuroplasticity—the formation and strengthening of the pathways in your brain related to your success. This may sound in alignment and synergistic with what was previously covered in the Visualization chapter in the Confidence section, but it works when we create such images in the minds of others, too.

Translating Ambition into Action

Just as extreme emotions (good or not so good) make events memorable for us, such as the birth of a child or when we get reprimanded by our boss, they can also be like superglue for our ambition to stick in the minds of others. For better or worse, emotions are what cement events in our minds and in the minds of others. When we are attempting to influence and gain buy-in, adding emotion to our ambition brings an otherwise hazy, non-existent, unmemorable reality for the other person into clear view, as if they are experiencing what we are suggesting.

Neville Goddard's assertion in The Feeling is the Secret rings true here—emotion is the lifeblood of ambition, the secret ingredient that can turn a well- crafted interaction into a call to action.

Imagine an important conversation that lies before you, such as a meeting with your boss or a presentation to your team. Picture its twists and turns: the setting, the stakeholders, the stakes. Envision the outcome with clarity and passion. Why does it matter? Who will it impact? Let these answers fill you with purpose, and let that purpose radiate outward. When you speak from this place of conviction, your words can do more than convey a message—they can lead others to mirror your vision.

Consider the relatively recent research in 2012 from the National Institute of Health about mirror neurons, which are cells in our brain that respond to actions that we observe in others. Miraculously, the research showed that mirror neurons fire in others the same way as when we recreate that action ourselves. So, you can imagine if we are nervous, uncertain, lacking confidence, frustrated, afraid, or annoyed, it could be problematic when trying to influence others.

Let us assume for a moment we've mastered being able to stay in the green on the Emotional Wheel, so negative emotions found deep in the yellow, or even worse, in the red, are off the table. That is so important, but the icing on the cake of being in the zone is being able to articulate what we are aspiring to accomplish with the positive emotion that will mirror the reaction that we'd like to have in others.

This is not to be unnatural or awkward. In other words, if you are reserved or soft-spoken, for example, your level of emotion when you are articulating your vision is a notch or two above where you normally are or where you feel comfortable. As a reminder, it is important to practice this in a safe or low-stakes environment first to see how it lands and for you to get comfortable being a little uncomfortable.

Have a colleague or family member rate how you are articulating your ask on a scale of 1 to 10, with 1 being extremely low energy and sounding doubtful, nervous, or frustrated, and 10 being confident and optimistic.

Are you merely reciting the plan that you learned, or are you kindling a flame? Your enthusiasm is like a light; let it shine brightly enough to guide others to your vision.

Even if, despite all your meticulous preparation, the response you receive is not as enthusiastic as you hoped, do not view it as a setback. Instead, see it as a step forward—a conversation that has begun to shift perceptions, laying the groundwork for future dialogue.

The Aspiration Articulator is a tool to help you prepare your mind and the minds of those you are looking to gain buy-in from. It will help others to see a future that involves them and one that is beneficial for them by mirroring how you'd like to feel as if what you are asking from your Challenge Builder Template has already transpired. The Aspiration Articulator Worksheet is a planning tool to consider the emotions we bring to the table for our ask as well as the emotions to create with the deal makers, those who are the main decision-makers, and the deal breakers (those who are potentially in the ear of the decision-maker).

Let's apply what we've learned in this section to an upcoming conversation that is important to you using the Aspiration Articulator™, so your aspiration is well thought out and the emotion of a bold vision is communicated and mirrored by your dealmaker and any potential dealbreakers.

Dealmaker: Who is the most important person that you'd like to influence and gain buy-in from?

_____

_____

_____

Dealbreaker: Who is someone who is potentially in the ear of the person you are trying to influence? They could be a colleague, board member, or even a friend/family member.

_____

_____

_____

How do I want to feel, and how do I want the person I'm influencing to feel when our conversation is over?

_____

_____

_____

How will I create the feeling I will leave them with?

_____

_____

_____

Here is a case study and example of a female leader who used what we've covered so far to showcase how ambition coupled with emotional regulation and strategic influence led to impactful outcomes.

Case Study: Finance Industry—Joan's Inclusive Leadership Initiative

Joan, a senior executive at a large investment bank, was determined to drive change within her firm to foster a more inclusive corporate culture. Her aspiration was to create a leadership training program specifically for women in the company to prepare them for their ascension to senior roles.

With contagious excitement, Joan presented her vision of how a diverse leadership team could lead to better decision-making and performance for the company. She highlighted the emotional and financial benefits of her initiative with compelling business cases and research on gender diversity in leadership.

Despite some initial resistance, Joan did not falter. When she was initially told there was no budget for such a program, she thanked her colleagues for their time and continued to collect data pointing to why such a program could help meet her boss's goals as well. By persistently showcasing her passion and the positive implications of her program, coupled with developing an E C O Mindset, she e v e n t u a l l y won over her leadership and initiated a successful executive development program for women.

This amazing female leader demonstrated how her aspiration was an important component of influence and could be harnessed to inspire and drive change. She showed that by connecting deeply with her vision and communicating it with clarity, emotion, and strategic preparation, she could bring about significant change in her company. Joan's story shows that when aspiration is fueled by genuine passion and commitment, as well as including others in that vision, it has the power to transcend barriers and create lasting impact.

Joan did not initially gain buy-in when she asked for the budget to support her program, but she understood that she had still made progress because she was able to influence her leadership about the business impact and share her vision for what a future favorable outcome could look like. During Joan's subsequent one-on-one with her boss the following month, she was able to secure 50 percent of the budget that she asked for. Joan was later told that the decision was made based on the research and facts that she provided but also because of her vision and commitment to see it through.

C H A P T E R   1 5

It's Time for Women to Become Even More Influential and Return to Power

Building influence so you can have a bigger voice, and impact is attainable regardless of your experience or title. There is also room for improvement for all of us. Building greater influence is not just a mighty goal. It is imperative that your voice can be heard, valued, and put into action by those in power who can champion your efforts. I believe with all my heart that women were meant to be in power. Putting aside my personal philosophy, there is evidence that the earliest leaders documented in history were women (Hastings, 2018). Anthropologists studying the rites and rituals of Paleolithic communities have discovered countless stone figurines of pregnant women across Europe, the Middle East, and India—some dating back to 25000 BCE—that point to the worship of the divine feminine. (Hastings, 2018).

If we continue our trip back in time to the ancient origins of human civilization, we find evidence that female deities were worshiped widely for millennia. Before current world religions were even established, during the earliest periods when humans were roaming the earth, many belief systems revered a supreme female creator. Ariana Grande references this belief in her song "God is a Woman," which has received over 178 million listens, not to mention roars at concerts, and archaeological evidence suggests that God was considered female for the first 200 thousand years of humans on earth (Hastings, 2018).

Considering today's civil unrest, war, and ego- driven behavior that is causing disruption with tragic consequences close to home and in far-off lands, it is imperative that women return to power and have a bigger voice within our companies and cultures to right the ship. I am not calling for the demise of the patriarchy as we need to work together with our amazing male allies to have the greatest impact, implement the greatest change, and sail through what is proving to be a stormy sea, arriving on the other side with hope, greater prosperity for all, and peace.

We're at an inflection point in history when women can learn to greet their fear, doubt, frustration, and anger with a new sense of gratitude, confidence, and power. We can break the present and generational shackles of cultural, social, and religious indoctrinations, which sometimes stand between our ability to speak up, be heard, and have the impact that we want and deserve; the impact that the world needs to see right now.

We can and we will.

But we'll need to be able to influence those in power who can provide rocket fuel and a tailwind for our efforts.

Are you in?

SHERYL KLINE, M.A. CHPC

C H A P T E R   1 6

For Our Amazing and
Invaluable Male Allies

To those who identify as male and stand as champions of women in their organizations, as well as embrace a feminine approach to leadership, your presence here is both commendable and critical. Your commitment to this journey of Fearless Female Leadership means we are making progress, signaling an era where support transcends gender and fosters a culture of collective empowerment.

In the landscape of business, the evidence is clear: Gender diversity is not just a moral imperative but a strategic advantage. According to their 'Why Diversity Matters' report (Hunt, Layton & Prince, 2015), McKinsey and Company reported that companies in the top quartile for gender diversity have a 15 percent return above national industry medians.

Further, "Without the avid support of men, often the most powerful stakeholders in most large corporations, significant progress toward ending gender disparities is unlikely," says Brad Johnson, professor of psychology in the Department of Leadership, Ethics, and Law at the United States Naval Academy.

However, truly championing the women in your circle of influence requires a nuanced understanding and a set of deliberate actions:

1. Cultural and Social Sensitivity

It's vital to appreciate the varied cultural and social norms that subtly shape workplace dynamics. Women often receive societal cues that discourage assertiveness and overt self-promotion. As an ally, you can play a transformative role by nurturing an environment that not only acknowledges but celebrates the achievements of women. Encourage women to articulate their accomplishments and take on new challenges with confidence. Such an environment not only uplifts the individuals but also enriches the collective intelligence and creativity of the team.

2. Allies for Our Amazing Allies

Embracing the role of an ally can sometimes feel like navigating uncharted waters, particularly in spaces where such efforts are nascent. The exchange of experiences and strategies among male allies is a treasure trove of wisdom, fostering a community that learns, adapts, and grows stronger together. It's about forging a path where allyship is the norm, and every step taken is a stride toward a more balanced and fairer workplace.

3. **Mastery of Tone**

Communication transcends the literal meaning of words to include the subtleties of tone and body language. Men and women may interpret and express emotional cues differently, so it's essential for male allies to develop a keen sense of awareness and adaptability in their interactions. Adopting an ECO mindset—embodying empathy, curiosity, and optimism—prepares you for interactions that are not just heard but felt. It's about establishing a dialogue that's grounded in understanding and respect, thus fostering a workplace where everyone feels valued and heard.

Becoming an ally is a journey of its own—a path of

introspection, learning, and action. It's about recognizing the impact of our words and actions on the women around us and taking proactive steps to support and elevate their voices. It's about understanding that allyship extends beyond moments of advocacy to everyday interactions and decisions.

The art of allyship is also about listening—truly listening to listen and not to respond—to the experiences and insights of women. It's about creating opportunities for their voices to lead conversations and shape decisions. It's about using your position to challenge biases, confront inequalities, and advocate for policies and practices that promote equity.

Dive into the resources available for allies. Seek out workshops, training sessions, and platforms designed to enhance your understanding and effectiveness as a supporter of gender diversity. Embrace the wisdom shared by thought leaders and advocates who have paved the way in allyship and diversity initiatives.

If you'd like to learn more about being an ally, I highly recommend the #ALLIES Journey on the Rali Change Experience Platform by the incredible Gavriella Schuster, former Corporate Vice President at Microsoft.

Your commitment as allies can bring about a transformation that transcends the workplace. It can shape a society where diversity is celebrated, where women's contributions are recognized and amplified, and where the next generation enters a world more equitable than the one we know today.

Through your unwavering support and active engagement, the goal of achieving a balanced and just workplace becomes more attainable. The journey toward equality is one we walk together, and your role as allies is not just supportive but foundational to this endeavor. Let's continue to build a future where ambition knows no gender, where leadership is defined by talent and vision, and where our collective efforts create a legacy of inclusion and empowerment.

Here are two case studies illustrating how male leaders from different sectors have become champions of female leadership and gender diversity.

Case Study: Technology Sector — Michael's Mentorship Program

Michael, the CEO of a midsize software company, recognized the gender gap in his development teams and the executive board. Determining that one of the best ways to support female professionals was through mentorship and sponsorship, he instituted a company-wide mentorship program aimed at identifying and nurturing female talent.

He personally took on the mentorship of several female leaders within the company, setting an example for other senior male staff. Michael's mentorship went beyond giving advice; he actively advocated for his mentees in leadership meetings, suggested them for high-profile projects, and supported their ideas in front of the entire company.

Under his leadership, the company saw a significant rise in female representation in managerial and executive roles and a resultant boost in innovation and market share, demonstrating the tangible benefits of male allyship in the tech industry.

Case Study: Academia—Professor James's Advocacy for Gender Balance

Professor James, a department head at an Ivy League university, noticed a concerning trend: While the student population in his department was fairly gender-balanced, the faculty was overwhelmingly male. He initiated a series of departmental reviews and workshops to address unconscious bias in hiring and promotion processes.

He then worked closely with the university's administration to create policies that provided equal opportunities for advancement and recognition for female academics. Professor James also ensured that female colleagues were equally represented on committees and in leadership roles within the department, leading to a more inclusive and balanced academic environment.

Case Study: Finance—Aaron's Inclusive Leadership Initiatives

Aaron, a senior partner at a large investment firm, was aware of the challenges female leaders faced in climbing the corporate ladder in finance. He established a Women in Leadership initiative that included networking events, leadership training, and a platform for women to present their business ideas to top management.

He also implemented transparent salary bands to address the pay gap and became a vocal advocate for flexible working arrangements to accommodate caregiving responsibilities—often a barrier for working women. Aaron's efforts resulted in a higher retention rate of female employees, more women in leadership roles, and an increase in female-led initiatives driving the firm's growth.

These case studies exemplify how male leaders can actively contribute to gender diversity and support female leaders. Through their actions, these men have not only advanced the careers of women but also enhanced the overall performance and culture within their respective organizations.

C H A P T E R   1 7

In Conclusion

The Fearless Female Leadership framework is a proven process and guidebook for you to ask and answer the questions, "What's my next level of impact?" "Where must my voice be heard, valued, and respected more?" You learned how to do this in the Clarity chapter by becoming the observer of your potential rather than a judge of your limitations.

You learned to fast-forward the movie about your impact to view it from your next finish line. You peeled back a layer or two of your highest sense of integrity and the legacy that you would like to create for yourself. Whether you aspire to have a bigger voice in your current role or to climb to new heights, you are now the Olympian who has clarity and an unwavering spark in your gut and in your heart for what must be done and for the message and mission you are committed to voicing.

You are a confident superhero now, wielding new power to get clear on what's next and accept your next level of impact with courage and confidence. In the Emotional Agility chapter, you learned how to regulate and use powerful emotions to your advantage, how to use Visual Optimization to imagine and eventually bring to life in your mind what is possible, and finally, how to create and sustain Momentum via setting up an accountability structure.

The Influence chapter is where you were able to prepare mentally and tactically to be a heard, valued, and respected change agent. Influencing is the key to the kingdom of change, and you now know how to do it in a way that is compassionate, respectful, and powerful.

Here's to you accessing the greatest gift of leadership and contribution that's been placed within you.

Cheering you on always and to your continued success,

If you'd like to contact Sheryl for Executive High-Performance Coaching, speaking, or corporate retainers, please email: info@sherylkline.com.

If you'd like to learn more about Sheryl, the leaders and organizations she's transformed:

SHERYL KLINE, M.A. CHPC

CHAPTER 18

Overview:
Wrap - Up

Today is the beginning of a new chapter! You stand at the threshold of untold possibilities, equipped with the insights and strategies that have propelled thousands of female leaders to the forefront of their industries. Embrace your vision, the clarity of your path, the confidence to see it through, and the influence to gain buy-in from those in power who can help you.

As we wrap up, let's reflect on the profound control you wield over your destiny. Your passion and expertise are the brushstrokes that paint your unique contribution to the world. Your voice is not just a whisper; it is part of a bigger picture to help with real change on your team, in your company, and, ultimately, in the world.

You started with a quest for Clarity. It was about more than setting goals—it was about aligning your work with your innermost values, identifying the essence of your authentic self, and setting a trajectory that resonates with your personal and professional ethos.

Remember the concept of Legacy? You envisioned the imprint you'd leave on your environment and thought deeply about how you'd want to be remembered. It's not just about the roles you'll fill but the lives you'll touch and the change you'll inspire.

Then came the exploration of Confidence, drawing parallels with the mental fortitude of athletes and visionaries. Like them, you've grappled with and overcome moments of self-doubt. This journey has rekindled your belief in your capabilities, reminding you that confidence is not static but a quality you can cultivate and grow.

Influence could very well be the cornerstone of this entire journey. Leadership, innovation, and change never occur in isolation. They come from collaboration, persuasion, and collective striving for a shared vision. You've learned to step into the minds of others, to see the world through their eyes, and to find the common ground that enables progress and consensus.

As you move forward, you can revisit the wisdom imparted in these chapters, use the worksheets to fine-tune your approach and rely on the robust framework you've built to amplify your presence and voice.

Let me reiterate what perhaps has not been said enough: Your voice is significant and highly valuable. It carries the weight of your experiences, your knowledge, and your unique perspective. I wholeheartedly believe in the boundless opportunities that lie ahead for your voice to be heard, valued, respected, and acted upon so you can be an even greater leader of change.

Carry forward the lessons of this journey with pride and conviction. And remember, with every step forward, you're not just advancing your career; you're paving the way for others to follow, setting a precedent for what it means to lead with integrity, vision, and an unwavering commitment to change.

For your ongoing Fearless Female Leadership journey, I stand beside you, cheering you on. The world awaits the impact you're destined to make, and I have no doubt you'll rise to meet it with the strength, grace, intelligence, and passion that you've demonstrated thus far. Here's to you, to your future, and to the indelible mark you'll continue to leave on your company and on the world!

SHERYL KLINE, M.A. CHPC

SHERYL KLINE, M.A. CHPC

Acknowledgments

Writing a book is like having kids. It's joyous, miraculous, uncomfortable, sometimes frustrating, and it takes a village. Coaching and mastermind colleagues, business mentors, family, friends, cheerleaders, structural editors, copy editors, my publisher Muse Literary, and the marketers (including my husband, Scott), who helped ensure this book marches towards helping one million women to have a bigger voice and access their highest sense of leadership and impact. For this, I am forever grateful.

This book was written in the midst of emotions; while selling a home that was a safe haven of comfort, healing, and joy after a rough patch in our lives. It was written during our quest to relocate from the San Francisco Bay Area to San Diego's North County in search of a vibe and a dream. Six moves in five months ensued while writing this book. The housing adventure was fun at first then not so much as we hopped from one Airbnb to the next with a one-month reprieve at our dear friends Shelley and Ron's home in Long Beach. For my best friend Pam, who was the constant voice of enthusiasm: "Keep going," "You can do it," "You're amazing,"

"Stop crying, you'll be OK"—thank you. You are my sister that I never had, and our daily calls and girls' trips sharing the triumphs, frustrations, tears, and joys are my lifeline.

For my mother, Barbara, you taught me and exemplified how to be kind. Your caring nature and compassion did not go unnoticed. It is my greatest sorrow that your voice was never heard, valued, or respected in our home or in the world. This book, my coaching practice working with women executives, emerging leaders, and my speaking engagements from stages large and small would never have happened if it were not for you. You are my muse and stand with me in all that I do and what I have become. Thank you for what you taught me, for continuing to stand beside me, and for helping me to be fearless. You are missed more than you'll ever know.

For Dad, you taught me that I can do whatever I put my mind to. You showed me that becoming a successful entrepreneur was possible. You showed me what commitment to family meant. I am forever grateful for your belief in me from as early as I can remember and for always making me feel important and loved. If I had one wish, it would be for you to be able to see your three, now adult, amazing grandkids. They would bring you so much joy, and you'd be so proud. Thank you for being the third leg of the tripod that held our family together, for having a sense of humor despite your circumstances, and for surviving when your plane was shot down in Yugoslavia during WWII. You were a model of resilience and mental toughness when you, as a Jew, were held as a prisoner of war in Germany for 40 days until the war was over. Through your stories, you showed me what mental toughness really is. I hope you are in Heaven smiling down on us. I miss you every day.

For my oldest son, Dan, I am so proud of the independent, kind, compassionate, brave, successful, and good-humored man you've become. You inspire me in the way you make bold decisions, see the good in everybody, and work hard, for the way others love you and value knowing you and for your willingness to go above and beyond in service to others. You consistently show up for family, and I cherish each time we can all get together. No one has named a tennis tournament after me like your last club did for you, so you must have left quite an impression before accepting a tennis pro role at the International Tennis Hall of Fame. Your caring and energy is felt and reciprocated. I love you. You are a gift.

For Ryan, I am so proud of your resilience, determination, and how you care deeply for others. From a young age, you were often told, "You can't." You can't be a Division I tennis player, you can't compete with players who are bigger and stronger than you, you can't get into the UC Berkeley Haas School of Business," etc. As it turns out, you absolutely can, you did, and you continue to trust your heart and your gut and work your butt off to get what you want and deserve. I am also inspired by how loyal you are to your family, friends, and colleagues, from checking in on birthdays and on random days, sending handwritten notes, flying in for Mother's Day, and the list goes on. I learn from you, and I appreciate you making the effort to stay connected. You are a great connector, always thinking of others, and you are well on your way to a tremendous impact on the world. You are a joy and an inspiration to me, and I am so proud of the young man you've become. I love you so much.

For the baby of the family, Megan. Where do I start? You are a resilient fighter who refuses to give up or back down from what you want to achieve. Your ability to have compassion and connect with others is a skill that's innate to you and one that's almost impossible to teach. You inspire me by how you are continually learning, growing, keeping the faith, and working hard for what you want and deserve. You, too, have not backed down when others doubted you. You may have been knocked out of the arena briefly at times, but you are always quick to dust yourself off and get back in. I am inspired by your dedication and resilience for what you want. You have so much to be proud of, including your amazing friends, your recent college graduation, and beginning to emerge as a leader in your first adulting job. I'm filled with joy for the caring, compassionate, and determined young woman you've become. Keep shining your light, and I can't wait for your adventures ahead. I am inspired by you, and I love you more than words can express.

For my structural editor, Mary, thank you for your honesty and expertise. You were the first one who took this book from a brain dump of information, research, and a framework to a coherent manuscript that can now be of service to others. You were able to see the good and the gaps in my writing. I am forever grateful for your expertise and encouragement.

For my thought leader, business mentor, and coach, Sara Connell, thank you for your guidance, knowledge, compassion, and caring, and for being a multi-million-dollar businesswoman who is changing lives and changing the world. You've exemplified what it means to show up in a world-class way, to genuinely care about those you work with, and how to forge a path to being a successful speaker, author, entrepreneur, and thought leader. For your guidance, expertise, and compassion, I am forever grateful.

For my coaching clients, past, present, and future, your willingness to do the work, exist outside your comfort zone, continue to learn and grow, and push the boundaries of what's possible inspires me daily. It's truly a gift to work with you and to know you. Your collective impact is vast and wide, changing history for the better.

For my husband, Scott, you are my rock, my biggest fan, and the one who provides irreplaceable support for me in my work and in life. Your caring heart, compassion, curiosity, fun-seeking personality, ability to connect with people (just about anywhere), and ability to love fiercely are truly uncommon and so special. You are ever the optimist and constant reminder that the world conspires for our success and that everything will work out in the best way possible. Your encouragement and tireless support behind the scenes have put wind beneath the sails of this book and behind the last 10 years of The Zone Lab's ability to empower thousands of female leaders and emerging leaders. My gratitude for you, your love, and your commitment to me and my kids is infinite.

SHERYL KLINE, M.A. CHPC

About Sheryl Kline

Sheryl Kline is a best-selling author, Forbes contributor, speaker, and CEO/Founder of The Zone Lab, LLC. She has worked with women in leadership and spoken on stages at Autodesk, Microsoft, VMware, Oracle, Bank of America, State Street Global Advisors, Jabra, and Commvault, to name a few. She lives in Carslbad, CA, with her husband, Scott and black lab, Kona.

www.sherylkline.com

SHERYL KLINE, M.A. CHPC

Bibliography
(Alphabetical Order)

Adapt for Life, 2024
https://www.adaptforlife.org/thoughts-feelings-behaviors#:~:text=%E2%80%9CThe%20way%20we%20think%20about,we%20present%20ourselves%20to%20others

Adapt for Life, 2024
https://www.adaptforlife.org/thoughts-feelings-behaviors#:~:text=%E2%80%9CThe%20way%20we%20think%20about,we%20present%20ourselves%20to%20others)

Ames and Mason, 2015
https://www.psychologicalscience.org/news/minds-business/offering-a-range-of-numbers-can-lead-to-an-edge-in-negotiations.html#:~:text=However%2C%20offering%20a%20range%20seems,ballpark%20as%20the%20initial%20offer.

Andersyn 2023
https://www.linkedin.com/pulse/impact-poor-emotional-intelligence-team-cohesiveness-andersyn-ph-d-/

Babcock and Laschever, 2003
https://www.amazon.com/Women-Dont-Ask-Negotiation-Gender/dp/069108940X

Bai, 2023
https://med.stanford.edu/news/all-news/2023/02/mirror-neurons-aggression.html#:~:text=Mirrors%20of%20rage&text=To%20set%20up%20a%20witness,qualifying%20them%20as%20mirror%20neurons

Blackmon, 2013
https://www.linkedin.com/pulse/science-behind-getting-out-our-comfort-zones-kelly-blackmon/

Bloomquist, 2024
https://www.linkedin.com/pulse/unlocking-power-no-oriented-questions-negotiations-molly-blomquist-twqpc/

Brouziyne and Molinaro, 2005
https://pubmed.ncbi.nlm.nih.gov/16350625/

Cherry, 2024
https://www.verywellmind.com/what-is-the-fight-or-flight-response-2795194

Derra, 2015
https://news.asu.edu/20151027-study-shows-angry-men-gain-influence-and-angry-women-lose-influence

Diversified Spaces, 2021
https://www.diversifiedspaces.com/2021/12/27/12-inventions-created-by-mistake/

Eikenberry, 2022
https://kevineikenberry.com/communication-interpersonal-skills/the-confidencecompetence-loop/#:~:text=As%20we%20become%20more%20skilled,work)%2C%20are%20forever%20joined

Gallo, 2022
https://www.melaniecgallo.com/single-post/why-we-don-t-like-surprises#:~:text=If%20the%20brain%20doesn't,of%20such%20an%20event%20occurring

Gastelum, 2021
https://www.police1.com/health-fitness/articles/why-our-brains-fixate-on-the-bad-and-what-to-do-about-it-hU18RitjpIsT4Moe/

Hampton, 2022
https://thebestbrainpossible.com/thoughts-brain-neuroplasticity-reality/

Harter, 2024
https://www.gallup.com/workplace/608675/new-workplace-employee-engagement-stagnates.aspx

Harvard Health Publishing, 2024
https://www.health.harvard.edu/healthbeat/the-nature-of-anger#:~:text=At%20the%20root%20of%20many,emotions%20often%20converge%20into%20anger

Hastings, 2018
https://www.vice.com/en/article/god-is-a-woman-history-goddess-worship-ariana-grande/

Hewlett, Marshal and Sherbin, 2013
https://hbr.org/2013/12/how-diversity-can-drive-innovation

History Extra, 2018
https://www.historyextra.com/100-women/100-women-results/?page=2

Hunt, Layton, and Prince, 2015
https://www.mckinsey.com/~/media/mckinsey/business%20f
unctions/people%20and%20organizational%20performance/o
ur%20insights/why%20diversity%20matters/why%20diversit
y%20matters.pdf

Kliner and Lemon, 2013
https://pmc.ncbi.nlm.nih.gov/articles/PMC3898692/

Lerner, Li, Valdesolo, and Kassam, 2014
https://pubmed.ncbi.nlm.nih.gov/25251484/

Lickerman, 2010
https://www.psychologytoday.com/us/blog/happiness-in-
this-world/201008/the-importance-of-
tone#:~:text=Whatever%20the%20content%20of%20the,tone%
20to%20which%20others%20respond

Little, 2021
https://www.history.com/news/coding-used-to-be-a-womans-
job-so-it-was-paid-less-and-undervalued

Markowsky, 2024
https://www.britannica.com/science/information-
theory/Physiology

Martin, 2024
https://www.psychologytoday.com/us/blog/conquering-codependency/202401/how-to-say-no-and-feel-good-about-it#:~:text=The%20Benefits%20of%20Setting%20Boundaries&text=Saying%20no%20allows%20us%20to,%2Dlove%20and%20self%2Drespect

McCloud, 2024
https://www.simplypsychology.org/maslow.html

Mether, 2023
https://www.fastcompany.com/90941598/3-ways-leaders-can-build-trust-and-connection-when-emotions-are-high

Neason, 2013
https://www.sportpsychologytoday.com/sports-psychology-articles/outcome-goals-vs-process-goals/

Neta and Kim, 2023
https://pmc.ncbi.nlm.nih.gov/articles/PMC10169535/

Olympic Channel, 2024
https://www.olympics.com/en/video/can-imagining-success-actually-help-you-achieve-it-olympic-state-of-mind

OSU.EDU, 2024
https://beyondpenguins.ehe.osu.edu/issue/icebergs-and-glaciers/all-about-icebergs

Parsons, 2007
https://www.reuters.com/article/world/angry-men-get-ahead-while-angry-women-penalized-study-idUSN01405185/

Popadopoulos, 2023
https://www.linkedin.com/pulse/power-precision-how-odd-numbers-boost-your-earnings-salary/

Reiners and Urwin, 2024
https://builtin.com/diversity-inclusion/diversity-in-the-workplace-statistics#0

Saplakoglu, 2023
https://www.quantamagazine.org/is-it-real-or-imagined-how-your-brain-tells-the-difference-20230524/#:~:text=Quanta%20Science%20Podcast,brain%20takes%20it%20for%20reality

Swaim, 2022
https://www.healthline.com/health/mental-health/how-does-emotion-impact-memory

Swaminathan, 2007
https://www.scientificamerican.com/article/women-talk-more-than-men/

Tartakovsky, 2018
Why Ruminating is Unhealthy and How to Stop
https://www.scribd.com/document/239771627/Why-Ruminating-is-Unhealthy-and-How-to-Stop-World-of-Psychology

Thornton, 2023
"Gadsden native Evelyn L. Lewis, track star, coach and mother of Olympic legend, dies at 93," Gadsden Times, January 9, 2023
https://www.gadsdentimes.com/story/news/2023/01/10/evelyn-lewis-mother-of-olympic-legend-carl-lewis-dies-at-93/69792170007/

Tyng, Amin, Saad, and Malik 2017
https://pmc.ncbi.nlm.nih.gov/articles/PMC5573739/

U.S. Army DEVCOM Army Research Laboratory Public Affair, 2020
https://www.army.mil/article/242062/army_researchers_acquire_two_new_supercomputers

SHERYL KLINE, M.A. CHPC

WITI, 2024
https://witi.com/halloffame/298369/ENIAC-Programmers-Kathleen-/

www.ingramcontent.com/pod-product-compliance
Lightning Source LLC
Chambersburg PA
CBHW030355130626
46549CB00004B/1505